Audience, Words, and Art

AUDIENCE, WORDS, AND ART

Studies in Seventeenth-Century French Rhetoric

By Hugh M. Davidson

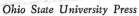

Ohio State University Press

To L. and A.

Preface

IN THE SIX STUDIES which make up most of the present volume, I have tried to do four things: (1) to recover the crucial steps in the attempt to reconstitute rhetoric as a discipline for France and for the French language in the seventeenth century (Chapters I–II); (2) to analyze the opposition to that attempt, as it appears in the *Logique* of Port-Royal (Chapters III–IV); (3) to show how Pascal, starting from principles like those of the Port-Royalists, invented an art of persuasion which is reflected in the *Lettres provinciales* especially, but also in the *Pensées* (Chapter V); and (4) to compare and contrast the ways in which one theme or factor in rhetorical theory—the audience—becomes specified in the minds of Corneille, Racine and Molière as they write and defend their dramatic works (Chapter VI). In a final chapter I have summarized my findings and have pointed out some of their literary implications in the seventeenth century.

In connection with the first of these aims, I have been obliged to choose from a multitude of relevant documents found in the Bibliothèque Nationale and elsewhere. The small number studied here have as a common feature a concern for rhetoric as a technical discipline that can be set down in a treatise; they are not occasional pieces that exemplify or use some particular aspect or device of rhetoric. My first two chapters contain, therefore, an account of the chief phases—translation, adaptation and reformulation—through which the ancient *scientia bene dicendi* passed in the period extending roughly from 1635 to 1685. It is here, perhaps, that the reason for the general title of this book is clearest, for at every turn in the theoretical study of rhetoric one encounters the three notions of audience, words, and art (in its personified form, speaker or writer), so interrelated that changes or effects in the first are traceable to causes in the other two, that is, in materials and techniques.

In my next main section, comprising Chapters III and IV, I have brought together and discussed evidence showing that Arnauld and Nicole intended to replace rhetoric by logic. Their project, based on Cartesianism, calls for innovation and for departure from tradition rather than for guidance from Aristotle, Cicero, and Quintilian, such as that sought by my first group of thinkers. As an intellectual center hostile to rhetoric, Port-Royal is thus set against the Academy, which was certainly the main base of those who wished to think and write according to lines laid down by ancient teachers of eloquence.

In treating seventeenth-century theorists and their Greek or Latin predecessors and in treating the conflict between the Port-Royalists and the upholders of the traditional rhetoric, my effort has been to go beyond confrontations on matters of detail. I have attempted to uncover principles and to give some sense of their consequences within the frameworks established by logic and rhetoric as disciplines. Such a treatment makes it possible for one to see through these seventeenth-century discussions to certain permanent possibilities of method that have not been, and indeed, cannot be, exhausted: for example, Rapin realized some of those possibilities in his particular way, as Quintilian had done in his fashion; and as later thinkers have shown, intellectual commitment and inventiveness are all that is needed for further elaborations. I have referred briefly to this point in Chapter IV; as a matter of fact, the somewhat paradoxical idea of rhetoric as a permanent possibility having various historical realizations underlies all that I have done here. (The same thing is true, of course, of logic.)

The relationship of disciplines or theories to literature is a delicate matter. Theories do not lead by some deductive process to works in their particularity, but they may explain the generic or common aspects of works, and beyond that, they define the field in or against which the author exercises his freedom of choice as to the end and means of his activity. I have studied this relationship in some detail in my two chapters on Pascal and on the major dramatists. To take the outstanding instance, the *Provinciales,* in certain of their fundamental characteristics, are what they are because of Pascal's geometrically inspired art of persuasion; he shows us what an intellectual position much like that of the authors of the Port-Royal logic will give when it is applied in a literary context. Similarly, one finds in the critical writings (essays, prefaces, epistles, and so on) of Corneille, Racine, and Molière many reminders of the rhetorical slant generally assumed by literary creation in the seventeenth century. I have studied one of these—the preoccupation with the audience and its tastes and its reactions—a propos of each of the dramatists and have found that each has his own manner of coping with his audience and, in his mind's eye, his own way of defining it. These two chapters (V and VI) present, therefore, two specifications in and around literature of principles drawn from seventeenth-century logic and rhetoric.

I am indebted to many friends and colleagues (at Dartmouth, at the Ohio State University, and elsewhere), with whom I have discussed almost everything that follows here; to the members of the committee who made it possible for me to spend a year in Paris as a Fulbright Research Scholar and to gather there the materials for Chapters I–IV; to Dartmouth College for grants to cover various incidental expenses; and to the Ohio State University for allowing me free time in which to complete this book. Without, of course, involving him in any way in the responsibility for my analyses and conclusions, I wish especially to acknowledge the assistance given me by Professor Richard McKeon, of the University of Chicago, whose penetrating essays and friendly suggestions have helped me a great deal.

H<small>UGH</small> M. D<small>AVIDSON</small>

Contents

Audience, Words, and Art

Chapter I

Problem and Solutions (I)

𝕴N SEVENTEENTH-CENTURY FRANCE the truly significant period of development for rhetoric begins in 1635 with the founding of the Academy. It is often wrong to emphasize dates in anything as complex and fluid as literary and intellectual history, but it is clear that in this case the date marks the start of a long alliance between rhetoric and official French policy. For the next fifty years, approximately speaking, no one could doubt the connection between the Academy and its program, on the one hand, and, on the other, what the monarchy and its ministers planned for France. Richelieu was, of course, the first patron of the group. In 1642, Pierre Séguier, *chancelier de France* and an intimate of the Cardinal, of Anne d'Autriche, and of Louis XIV, succeeded to the post. Thirty years later, at the death of Séguier, Louis XIV declared himself the protector of the Academy and set aside a place in the Louvre for its *séances*. Colbert interested himself directly in its work: it is known that he tried to stimulate its members to greater zeal and speed in their tasks than they sometimes showed. To recall these names is enough to indicate the kind of support given to the institution and the degree of importance attached to its program.

From the outset, the work of the Academy—as one may

3

see from the *lettres patentes,* the first deliberations, the early discourses read at the meetings, and from other references—was linked in one way or another with the notion of *éloquence*. In the official documents, Louis XIII declared: "Qu'après avoir fait tant d'exploits mémorables nous n'avions plus qu'à ajouter les choses agréables aux nécessaires, et l'ornement à l'utilité; et qu'il [Richelieu] jugeait que nous ne pouvions mieux commencer que par le plus noble de tous les arts, qui est l'éloquence."[1]

The term reappeared as the members sought to define their task: "Dès la seconde assemblée, sur la question qui fut proposée de sa fonction [i.e., de l'Académie], M. Chapelain représenta qu'*à son avis elle devait être de travailler à la pureté de notre langue; et de la rendre capable de la plus haute éloquence. . . .*"[2] In his *projet,* Chapelain repeated his view that the aim of the Academy was to make eloquence possible—this time it is "la dernière éloquence"—and went on to say that two ample treatises were needed, a rhetoric and a poetic. These would provide rules for writers in prose and in verse. But it would be impossible to compose them until a treatise on grammar was ready, since the grammar, as he conceived it, would furnish the body of the language, the necessary basis to which one might add the "ornaments of oratory and the figures of poetry."[3] Moreover, prior to all these tasks lay that of compiling a dictionary, a treasury of elements out of which the rest could be constructed. As is evident, the idea of a cumulative series is what gives the plan its force: each of the verbal disciplines furnishes, by the investigation of its characteristic problems, the bases of the following one. At one end of the sequence is a collection of words tested but as yet unused (theoretically speaking); at the other end is the kind of knowledge (that is, poetics) needed for the most elaborate kind of expression.

The efforts to realize this logical scheme met over the

4

years many obstacles: the irregular schedule of the *séances*; poor attendance; the unwieldiness of the group; the pull of activities other than those outlined in the program; the criticisms and ironies of those on the "outside." But finally, after an interval of approximately sixty years, the Dictionary appeared in 1694. The preface of that work recalled the original program, without making any promises as to when the series of treatises would be finished.

One might conclude, therefore, that the grammar, the rhetoric, and the poetics had not been and never would be realized: the grand undertaking had failed.

However, I believe it possible to say, without simply indulging in paradox, that the whole plan had been effectively carried out. The official grammar, rhetoric, and poetics, in so far as they were write-able at all, had been composed through a curious combination of logic and favorable circumstances. Obviously the realization of the tasks could not wait until 1694 or thereafter. By that time basic moral and artistic attitudes had undergone a change. Leading critics were moving toward what was to become the Encyclopedists' conception of art works as products of the imagination. The terms of the discussion were arising out of psychological rather than technical considerations. Moreover, Louis XIV's regime, no longer a stable background against which literature might emerge as a splendid ornament, provided more and more subjects for critical analysis and for satire.

But to return to my main point: the intellectual task of realizing treatises on language and its literary uses had been done, not by the Academy as a group, but by *individuals* who were members of it or who worked obviously from the starting points that Chapelain had originally outlined.[4] In other words, there was in the middle decades of the century a widely-held view, more an attitude than a theory, that had been made explicit by the Academy. As I have suggested, it is

5

the conviction that literature is work with words according to distinct methods that lend themselves to explicit and even systematic treatment.[5] To those who wished to pursue the matter further, this constituted a way of asking the questions; and writers like Vaugelas, Rapin, Boileau, and Bouhours worked out as best they could—*as individuals*—the consequences of this basic attitude.

Vaugelas' *Remarques sur la langue française* of 1647 falls on the borderline between grammar and rhetoric. One will not find in it, of course, anything like a systematic presentation of the topics associated with grammar, although many of the materials for such a treatment are definitely present, and Vaugelas himself believes that he has given answers to the outstanding questions of word forms and syntax. The strong emphasis on usage, which he describes in the Preface as "the King, the tyrant, the arbiter, the master of languages," indicates clearly the grammatical aspect or tendency of his work. He thinks of himself, not as a legislator, but as a witness, one who wishes to describe, in his well-known phrase, ". . . la façon de parler de la plus saine partie de la cour, conformément à la façon d'écrire de la plus saine partie des auteurs de ce temps."[6] I do not mean to imply, of course, that his description is purely objective or purely factual. The quotation shows his normative bias; and where the facts fail him, he falls back on reason, that is, where usage is doubtful, he argues by analogy from it in order to arrive at a preferred word or form.

The real centers of interest for him, however, take him over the boundaries of grammar into rhetoric. The two technical notions in the light of which he works are *pureté* and *netteté* of language. These two qualities are the bases of elo-

6

quence, he tells Séguier in the dedicatory epistle, and he restates the point many times before the *Remarques* are concluded. In other words, he is looking beyond grammar to the ultimate use of language; or, to put it in another way, in writing his grammar, he looks for guidance toward rhetoric, a discipline higher on the scale of verbal arts. As a matter of fact, it is obvious that Quintilian, *the* teacher of eloquence, is at the origin of Vaugelas' distinction.

> Un langage pur, est ce que Quintilien appelle *emendata oratio* et un langage net, ce qu'il appelle *dilucida oratio*. Ce sont deux choses si différentes, qu'il y a une infinité de gens, qui écrivent nettement, c'est-à-dire clairement et intelligiblement en toutes sortes de matières, s'expliquant si bien qu'à la simple lecture on conçoit leur intention, et néanmoins il n'y a rien de si impur que leur langage. [*Remarques*, pp. 577–78.]

Again, in his long article on *équivoques*, Vaugelas refers specifically to Quintilian's chapter "De perspicuitate" in Book VIII of the *Institutio oratoria*. And for another clear sign of the degree to which the rhetorical vocabulary dominates the thinking of Vaugelas, note the diction of the following lines from the Preface, where he lists subjects an author might have treated in connection with the French language. The leading ideas appear in the traditional, cumulative order that runs from correctness through elegance to rhythm.

> Après cela il eût encore fait voir qu'il n'y a jamais eu de langue où l'on écrit plus purement et plus nettement qu'en la nôtre, qui soit plus ennemie des équivoques et de toute sorte d'obscurité, plus grave et plus douce tout ensemble, plus propre pour toute sorte de styles, plus chaste en ses locutions, plus judicieuse en ses figures, qui aime plus l'élégance et l'ornement, mais qui craigne plus l'affection. Enfin il eût fait voir qu'il n'y en a point qui observe plus le nombre et la cadence dans ses périodes, que la nôtre, en quoi consiste la véritable marque de la perfection des langues. [Préface, *Remarques*, p. 3, § xv.]

A similar passage occurs at the end of the *Remarques,* in the very last paragraph, in fact:

A la pureté, et à la netteté du style, il y a encore d'autres parties à ajouter, la propreté des mots et des phrases, l'élégance, la douceur, la majesté, la force, et ce qui résulte de tout cela, l'air et la grâce, qu'on appelle le je ne sais quoi, où le nombre, la brièveté et la naïveté de l'expression, ont encore beaucoup de part. [*Remarques,* p. 593.]

The tying of purity and clarity of language on to the order of stylistic qualities traditionally followed by the rhetoricians is already unmistakable, but Vaugelas goes on to make the connection explicit. It is not for him, he says, to treat these other subjects: they exceed his powers; they require no less than a "Quintilien français." At the end of the Preface, just after the lines I have quoted above, he returns to the need for such a master. In fact, Vaugelas has a candidate in mind.

He allows himself a short nominating speech, tactfully omitting, however, the name of the nominee: "La gloire en est réservée toute entière à une personne qui médite depuis quelque temps notre rhétorique, et à qui rien ne manque pour exécuter un si grand dessein. . . . " Vaugelas' period flows on. His candidate is a product of Athens and Rome, as well as of Paris; his eloquence bears the mark of the best minds of those three famous cities; he is one of the great ornaments of the bar and of the Academy, one whose tongue and whose pen are equally eloquent. . . . "C'est celui qui doit être ce Quintilien français, que j'ai souhaité à la fin de mes *Remarques*" (Préface, *Remarques,* p. 3, § XV).

In summary, then, one may say that the *Remarques* of Vaugelas stem directly from the conception of literary disciplines which the Academy had expressed in its early plans.[7] Although his work does, indeed, fall mainly in the domain of grammar, he defines or understands grammar as the basis

8

of rhetorical elaboration. Occasionally he touches on subjects usually associated with rhetoric. Still, he feels that the big questions there, especially those dealing with the beauties of elocution, will have to be treated by another hand. And, as we have seen, he knows someone "qui médite depuis quelque temps notre rhétorique."

Pellisson and d'Olivet furnish in their history the key to the identity of the man Vaugelas had in mind. He was Olivier Patru, an *avocat au Parlement,* who was received into the Academy in 1640. A lawyer who had once had great success at the bar, he became, as time passed, more and more preoccupied with language and letters. He is supposed to have helped Vaugelas with his *Remarques.*[8] He was an important collaborator, along with Rapin and Bouhours, on the *Dictionnaire* of Richelet. According to Bouhours, whose opinion is reported by Pellisson and d'Olivet, he was " . . . l'homme du Royaume qui savait le mieux notre langue." [9] And he knew it not simply as a grammarian, but as an orator, we are told.[10] The passage at the end of Vaugelas' Preface, from which I have quoted above, is recalled:

> Une si rare louange s'adresse à M. Patru; et c'est lui qui devait être ce Quintilien français, que Vaugelas souhaite à la fin de ses remarques.
> On le regardait effectivement comme un autre Quintilien, comme un oracle infaillible en matière de goût et de critique. Tous ceux qui sont aujourd'hui nos maîtres par leurs écrits se firent honneur d'être ses disciples. [*Histoire,* II, 177.]

The reputation of infallibility is somewhat shaken for us by two bits of advice that Patru gave. He is the "maître de notre éloquence" to whom La Fontaine refers in the preface to his fables,[11] and this master, on hearing of La Fontaine's plan of doing his fables in verse, warned the poet against

9

the idea, because he believed that the genre required something like the brevity and dryness of Aesop's prose. On another occasion, he advised Boileau that the art of poetry could not be elaborated in a poetic form: it was not a "matière susceptible d'ornement" (*Histoire,* p. 178).

Indeed, where his own work was concerned, Patru seems to have been a victim of this critical and negative temperament. Nothing ever came of his plan to produce the French rhetoric. At his death, a *projet informe* was found, but that was all. "Il n'était pas homme d'un grand travail," say Pellisson and d'Olivet, and they add: "D'ailleurs le soin excessif qu'il apportait à la correction de ses ouvrages, lui donnait le temps de vieillir sur une période. Le mal est que ses affaires domestiques en souffrirent, et qu'à la fin il fut durement vexé par ses créanciers." [12]

If Patru had lived up to the expectations of Vaugelas and had composed a rhetoric that was authentically French, he would no doubt have had even more influence than he seems to have had, anyway. He embodied the aspiration of the Academy toward regular eloquence. He worked to revive and continue the ancient rhetorical tradition—too piously, one may say, and yet not without tact or independence. No one knows precisely what his doctrine was or might have been. However, we find some indication of it in a letter to the "Révérend Père *** de la compagnie de Jésus" that is published in his *Oeuvres.*

In this letter he takes up an important subject: the very possibility of *éloquence* in the seventeenth century. It had been argued that neither the materials nor the occasions for oratory such as that of Demosthenes or Cicero existed any longer. Patru replies that a certain degree of moral and intellectual development, that is, a particular state of *moeurs* and of *esprits,* must be present for it: this is presupposed by all the rest, since it results in efforts to cultivate and perfect language. That said, he takes up the terms of the argument. He claims that the subjects and opportunities for the three ancient types of oratory—judicial, deliberative, and demonstrative—do still exist. He even emphasizes the possibility of deliberative oratory, although he is obliged to admit that the political regime under which he lives differs widely from that of the ancient republics in which deliberative oratory had flourished. Furthermore, we need to recognize, he says, that we have in France possibilities that Cicero and Demosthenes did not have: the subjects and techniques of *l'éloquence de la chaire.* Then, with what seems to be at least a partial return to his original point—the importance of moral and intellectual culture—he writes: "Enfin je conclus de tout cela que si nous n'avions point d'éloquents, ce n'est ni faute de matière, ni faute d'occasion, mais faute ou d'esprit ou de travail." [13]

According to Pellisson and d'Olivet, the model he set for himself was Cicero, and they allow him all the virtues of his model except "force et véhémence." His gentleness of character precluded these qualities, they say in his defense, adding an amiable *non sequitur* to the effect that one must consider the many vices of which he had to purge French eloquence. And so, if the age did not have a Quintilian in the form of a treatise, it did have one in the flesh, and just missed having a Cicero, too.

There were a number of other and more tangible attempts to solve the problem of rhetoric as a discipline to be constituted. The subsequent history of eloquence in the seventeenth century provides, in fact, an interesting example of the way in which an intellectual question or need comes to be widely felt and then acted upon. The logic of the underlying literary theory posed the problem with unmistakable clarity. But, to be effective, logic had to have help from accidents of birth, training, and circumstance: it was necessary to wait for the appearance of an individual able to bring about a solution in the form of a *treatise*. That was the natural response to make to the challenge, it seemed, in an age that tended to believe strongly in the value of formally conceived arts and sciences.

Eventually two treatises did appear, one in 1659 and the other in 1671, both claiming to fill the need that had been indicated. What was called for was so obvious that they even had identical titles: *La Rhétorique française*. The first was written by René Bary, *conseiller et historiographe du Roi*, the second by the Sieur Le Gras, *avocat au Parlement*.[14]

Each of these works is placed explicitly in the continuing stream of concern for eloquence. The fulsome introduction to the treatise of Bary, signed by Le Grand, sieur des Herminières, another royal counselor and member of the bar, mentions the "promise" of the Academy and the hopes centering on Patru:

> Je ne crois pas, Monsieur, offenser votre modestie, si je dis que c'est à vous seul, à qui notre siècle doit entièrement l'élégance du discours et la beauté de l'éloquence. . . . Il y a longtemps que la célèbre Académie, la gloire du Royaume, et la maîtresse de l'éloquence, nous avait fait la promesse d'une Rhétorique si souhaitée. Mais enfin, Monsieur, votre libéralité l'en a pleinement acquittée: et nous attendrons avec moins d'impatience que l'éloquent Patru joigne sa magnificence à votre libéralité, et, qu'il y ajoute l'excès de ses trésors à l'abondance de vos richesses.[15]

Jean-Louis Guez de Balzac, he goes on to say, was the first to achieve uniformity of style in the French language and to discover its possibilities for periodic rhythms, but he credits Bary as being the first to formulate the rules with certainty. "C'est pourquoi les plus vains et les plus envieux sont contraints d'avouer que votre Rhétorique doit régner dans l'empire des belles-lettres" (Bary, p. xxxi).

In his turn, Le Gras refers twelve years later to previous efforts to compose a French rhetoric and to the end of Vaugelas' Preface. The author of the *Remarques*, as capable as anyone of doing the job, he says, had left it for someone else who had been meditating on it for a long time and who had all the needed qualifications. "Mais cette rhétorique prétendue étant demeurée sans éclore depuis vingt-quatre ans qu'elle a été promise; cela nous doit faire croire que la mort de l'auteur, ou quelque autre accident nous a dérobé cet avantage." [16] He obviously intends to challenge the "reign" of Bary's treatise "in the empire of belles–lettres." He knows his predecessor's work, to judge from the slighting remarks he makes about a rhetoric " . . . qui a paru au jour depuis quelques années," and from a passage that he quotes disapprovingly from Le Grand's extravagant introduction. But he evidently has decided to dismiss all previous work as unfruitful and as too general.

When we turn to the examination of these two arts, we see some, but not much, originality in the treatments of the subject. The authors do attempt to write specifically French rhetorics. They know that they must describe the circumstances in which eloquence may occur in France in the seventeenth century, circumstances necessarily different from those to which the classical theories were adjusted. Whenever they think of their subject matter in relatively narrow terms, that is, when they think of it primarily as oratory, they tend to substitute for the ancient division (deliberative, judicial and demonstrative or epideictic oratory) the distinction of eloquence into that of the *chaire* and that of the *barreau*. They emphasize the novelty of Christian eloquence, although they see in Augustine, if not in their pagan masters, Cicero, Quintilian, and Aristotle, a patron and source of instruction. The differences in the geniuses of the languages are given

13

special and usually short treatments: French has resources not available to Greek and Latin, and vice versa. In the main, these comments are grammatical rather than rhetorical.

On the whole, the two treatises are best thought of as redoings of Quintilian, with help from his predecessors and followers. That of Le Gras is more comprehensive in this way. His work is only an *abrégé*, he says, although it contains the main precepts of Aristotle, Cicero, Quintilian, Hermogenes, Augustine, Scaliger, Erasmus, Vossius, "et plusieurs autres." (In the seventeenth century, *plusieurs* usually equals *beaucoup*.) Principally, though, he follows Quintilian, who, in the opinion of all those who know, was the "most excellent" master or teacher of rhetoric in Rome. But in the cases of both Bary and Le Gras, it is clear that they are translating, paraphrasing, and popularizing a doctrine already in existence, already having its classic exposition. In so doing, they obviously make a real contribution to the vitality of the dominant view of literature and the way in which it is composed. And yet one must say more, I think, than that they repeat effectively, along with inevitable variation and some originality, what they find in their models. Their sense of the tradition they represent has to be grasped apart from the details of their treatises. What counts for more is their way of conceiving the doctrine as a whole and its relations to other disciplines. Bary's prefacer makes very broad claims:

> Véritablement, l'art de bien dire, et la souveraine éloquence dont je parle, est la plus importante pièce de la Politique; puisque c'est elle qui enseigne à persuader les esprits et à fléchir les volontés dans les cabinets des Princes, dans les compagnies souveraines, dans les temples et dans les armées.[17]

Le Grand does not limit the place and power of rhetoric to the practical decisions of politics. Taking up the Ciceronian ideal of a wedding of wisdom and artistic expression, he finds a place in philosophy for his discipline, not merely as a method of exposition, but also as a method leading to the solution of problems. Perhaps the most interesting assertion, for the student of seventeenth–century literature, is the one that locates rhetoric between dialectic and poetry. It may use the reasoning techniques of the former while avoiding its abstractness and technicality; and it may use rhythm or *nombre* without precise counting of syllables. It is easy, within this framework, to move rhetoric toward either of the extremes. Having first provided himself with a classical precedent, Le Grand turns first toward poetry and then toward logic.

> Nous pouvons encore parler plus nettement, et nous pouvons dire avec le Stoïque Posidonius que la poésie est une oraison nombrée, qui n'est différente de la rhétorique que par la proportion de certaines mesures, et que par l'excès de quelques licences; que ces mesures et ces excès ne donnent point d'atteintes ni de changements à la substance de la chose; et que la rhétorique peut subsister non seulement dans le nombre des fictions poétiques et figurées, mais aussi dans la méthode des syllogismes épidictiques ou contentieux. [Bary, pp. vii–viii.]

Here is surely an interesting variation from our original set of terms—dictionary, grammar, rhetoric, poetic—where precise relationships were not expressed. There was a sequence, foreseen in the program, as I have noted, since each of the later treatises would depend on the earlier one or ones. But here we learn first of rhetoric as a tool in politics and in philosophy, where it is widely applicable, and then as a productive art of discourse which takes its place between dialectic (or logic) and poetry. The mean term differs from the extremes only in degree. This is especially true where poetry is involved: " . . . concluons hardiment que la poétique n'est autre chose, que la partie la plus contrainte et la plus observée de l'art oratoire" (Bary, p. viii). It is reasonable, therefore, to say with Cicero that Homer was a great orator, with Hermogenes that he was an excellent rhetorician, and with Demetrius that he was *the* teacher of eloquence.

Le Grand qualifies this abstract view of poetics as a part of rhetoric. As things happened in history, he believes, the natural movement was from poetic eloquence, with its original burden of laws, moral principles, religious mysteries, and secrets of nature, to the looser discipline of eloquence itself. By the discovery of the principles of rhetoric, the human mind managed to disengage speech from the rules of poetry. He applies this myth to the history of French language and literature: in the sixteenth and seventeenth centuries he sees the flowering of poetry as leading to the perfecting of prose, as opening the way to such things as elegance and ornament. (The treatise of Bary could then appear as the climax of this evolution in French thought and expression!)

Le Gras is hardly less bold in his claims for rhetoric. In his dedication, which is addressed to Colbert, he says concerning the worth of his subject:

C'est, Monseigneur, le plus important de tous les arts, la plus relevée de toutes les sciences humaines, qui enseigne à faire servir les autres sciences au commerce de la vie civile, au bien et au salut des hommes; les détourner de leurs mauvaises entreprises; les consoler dans leurs afflictions; les soutenir dans leurs défaillances; et les relever de leur abattement et de leur chute. Elle montre comment il faut défendre leurs biens, leur vie et leur honneur. Enfin cet art contient les règles nécessaires pour défendre la vérité, et la faire triompher du mensonge. C'est ce qui lui a fait donner le titre glorieux de Reine des Sciences.[18]

A little later he adds that this queen of the sciences is also the most stately and magnificent ornament of any empire.

He tells, in his preface, of two enthusiasms that motivate him. He admired Quintilian as the teacher of rhetoric and he admired Colbert for his efforts to equal the achievements, or more exactly the ornaments, of the Greek and Roman "empires." Since the greatest of the ornaments is eloquence, he felt himself obliged to treat of that art, and to do so according to the example of the Latin master.

In spite of these claims, one senses a defensive tone here and there in the Preface. Many people misunderstand the position of his science, he says; they put rhetoric after the other disciplines instead of before and above them. This inadequate conception causes young men to be prejudiced against it, to scorn "cet art excellent de la parole." He tries, therefore, to explain why the ancients held it in high favor and why he wants to help it regain its prestige.

All this indicates, I think, that by 1670 we are reaching a critical point in taste and in theorizing about eloquence. Le Gras has composed a treatise based on a model that has lost some of the magic it had twenty years before. As we shall see, Rapin is already putting together at this same time a treatment of eloquence that is not only more independent in spirit than that of Le Gras but also more flexible and accessible than that of Quintilian. And so Le Gras finds himself presenting his work to a generation that is somewhat indifferent to the claims and technicalities of rhetoric. But he remains convinced of its educative value. He sees it as inseparable from moral virtue—the theme is the ancient one of the *vir bonus dicendi peritus*, fully developed by Quintilian—and he concludes: "En un mot, il n'y a point d'ouvrage dans toute l'Antiquité plus capable d'éclairer l'esprit, de former le jugement, ni de rendre un homme habile et capable des plus grandes choses que les institutions oratoires de Quintilien" (Préface, *La Rhétorique française*, p. xxi).

Although these epistles and prefaces belong to genres which

encourage an inflationary attitude toward the subject at hand, they are nevertheless revealing. In them one gets a feeling for the connotations and associations that the art of rhetoric had at the time when they were composed and, also, a sense of individuality in point of view, whereas, once the technical parts of the works begin, the sequence of topics follows that of Quintilian and Cicero. But I should like in any case to review briefly the method and central notions of Le Gras; I choose him because he is more orderly and thoroughgoing than Bary.

He starts with an elaborate definition of rhetoric as it is seen from five different angles: according to the etymology of the word (this takes him back to ῥέω, ῥήτωρ and ῥητορική); according to the essence of the doctrine (for him expressed as "l'art de bien dire"); according to the effects of the art (it aims to change or dominate minds through the power of speech); according to its parts (it directs the processes of invention, arrangement, expression, retention, and delivery); and according to the divisions of the speech itself (it gives rules for conciliating the audience in the exordium, for instructing it in the narration and in the proofs, and for exciting suitable emotions in the peroration). And he reverts to the requirement I have already mentioned, that the orator must be an *homme de bien*, " . . . parce que la rhétorique donnant des règles pour traiter un sujet des deux côtés, il faut nécessairement que celui qui possède cet art, soit homme de bien, pour ne s'en servir qu'à faire triompher la vérité et la justice" (*La Rhétorique française*, pp. 2–3).

The method falls into four parts for Le Gras (since he puts into a single section both memorization and delivery). Under the heading of invention, we meet again the inevitable distinction of the three genres—demonstrative, deliberative, and judicial—which include all possible subjects of discourse. Le Gras, himself a lawyer, analyzes the last type in detail, treating of the *lieux*, the kinds of questions, the problem of the passions and how to arouse them. For disposition or arrangement, he goes back to the consecrated terms used in his definition and writes a section on exordium, narration, and so forth.

Then comes elocution. Le Gras repeats and develops two things that he had already said in a passage of the preface, a passage that obviously echoes Vaugelas and Quintilian, namely, that elocution or expression is the most important and the most difficult part of rhetoric, and that the fundamental qualities one must seek are *pureté* and *netteté* in language.[19] The first of these refers, of course, to the *sine qua non* of grammatical correctness. *Clarté* or *netteté* concerns the applications of words to things; it depends on the propriety of language; and here Le Gras enters on a long sevenfold discussion of how one determines when words are *propres* or not.

After these basic virtues or qualities, the writer must look to ornamentation, which is taken to be the most important part of rhetoric. Since ornamentation is what holds the attention of the listeners and produces admiration in their minds, one cannot call eloquent any discourse that lacks it, no matter how pure the diction may be or how clear the expression. An ornament or figure is any uncommon form of expression; applied to a single word, it is a *trope* (as metaphor or onomatopoeia); to more than one word, it becomes either a *figure de mots* (as antithesis or anaphora) or a *figure de pensée* (such as interrogation or doubt). Le Gras insists on the need to integrate ornamentation into the fabric of the discourse. One does not use it for its own sake. It gives to variety style; it makes the subject matter vivid; it affects the emotions of the listener or reader; it serves to render the emotions of the speaker and hence to promote conviction; it provides, in some cases, useful transitions; and finally, it makes possible the *genre sublime*.

19

When he moves on to the subject of "composition," Le Gras tries to do something new in French. He understands by this term the final fitting together of the speech, especially as regards details in the sequence of ideas, words, and sounds. This gives him his occasion to treat the qualities of discourse that are subject to the judgment of the ear. Before him, he claims, no one had discussed composition in this sense. But he will attempt it, since Cicero had asserted that the beauty of an oratorical piece consists not only in the exactness of the words and in the magnificence of the ornaments, but also in the final disposition of the words and in their metrical characteristics. Here Le Gras borrows a distinction from Quintilian —*ordo, junctura,* and *numerus,*[20] which he renders as *ordre, liaison,* and *nombre. Ordre* has to do typically with gradation or climax or prerogative in a sequence of ideas. In a developing expression, for example, he recommends that we normally mention day before night and man before woman! Under *liaison,* the typical concern is to remove clashes of vowels or other harsh combinations of sounds, so as to leave with the listener an impression of smoothness and fullness. Finally *nombre,* a quality depending again on the judgment of the ear, refers to the introduction of measure into discourse. It must not, however, resemble in a strict way the measure of French verse: in prose, verses are a great vice. Le Gras calls this effect *rime,* after the Greek ῥυθμός, he says. He points out the ambiguity of the term and the possibility of confusion with the end rhymes of French verse. This metrical discussion leads to a short section on periods, since the rhetorical period is composed of members having some resemblance to verses.

The chapter heading "De la bienséance ou manière de parler juste" signals a new and important turn in the exposition. Le Gras recalls the opinion of Cicero that this is one of the most important and difficult parts of rhetoric. "En effet, la bienséance est ce qui donne plus de grâce et de force à l'oraison: tellement que le même Cicéron dit que celui qui la sait ménager dans le discours, mérite avec justice le titre glorieux d'orateur" (*La Rhétorique française*, p. 239). The phrase *parler juste* indicates the turn the argument is taking. Up to this point, the treatise has given the principles of speaking well, of *parler bien*. The new phrase adds to the idea of an intrinsic excellence in thought and expression still another quality, the suitability of the speech to factors outside of itself, to the audience and to the circumstances in which it will be said or read. "La bienséance a quelque rapport au devoirs de la civilité, au compliment et à la politesse: tellement que ceux qui n'ont pu s'en servir, sont rustiques et sauvages" (*La Rhétorique française*, p. 239). I shall not go here into the various divisions of *bienséance*, as it applies to subject matters, ends, manners, person, times, and places, but I should like to quote from a page where Le Gras contrasts and relates *utilité* and *bienséance*:

> Avant de pouvoir achever ce traité, il est nécessaire de remarquer en cet endroit que celui qui veut parler juste, doit prendre garde que ce qu'il dit soit non seulement utile à son sujet, mais aussi bienséant: que ces deux parties sont souvent unies, parce que ce qui est bienséant est pareillement utile: qu'il arrive néanmoins quelquefois que ces parties sont opposées, et qu'alors la bienséance doit prévaloir, et obliger à se taire, dont on apporte l'exemple de Socrate, qui aima mieux souffrir la mort par une condamnation injuste, que de se servir de l'oraison que Lysias avait dressée pour sa défense. . . . [*La Rhétorique française*, pp. 243–44.]

What the subject demands and what the occasion demands may come into conflict. When they do, Le Gras is ready to decide the issue in favor of the latter.

He ends his treatment of elocution with the traditional

distinction of the *style bas*, the *style médiocre*, and the *style sublime*. In a series of analogies or parallels, he first refers the styles to the three aims of speech: to instruct, to please, and to move. He then assigns to each a typical subject matter: relatively unimportant topics like material things or money, matters that are "médiocres"—Le Gras obviously has some difficulty with this mean term; he repeats it without examples —and finally matters of life and death, of state and religion. He attempts a differentiation of effects: the hearer follows the discourse ("se laisse aller au discours") in the first two types or he is moved to tears or other signs of strong feeling in the sublime genre. Le Gras thinks that the styles should be mingled for variety and relief; in fact any speech, as he conceives it, tends to go through the three styles in succession, instructing, pleasing, and moving by turns. It should be said in his favor, after this confused and inadequate formulation of a complex matter, that Le Gras recognizes the possibility of changes and variations in this order and adds a qualification to the effect that one very rarely finds an orator equally good in all three styles.

I have described first the method of Le Gras, although it came after that of Bary, because the values and weaknesses of the earlier work stand out by comparison. Bary's treatise is less complete and less orderly; one can understand the feeling of Le Gras that *the* French rhetoric had not yet been written as he surveyed what his predecessors—and in particular, Bary—had done. For example, Bary treats only of invention, disposition, and expression, whereas Le Gras, with more pious regard for his sources, restores memorization and delivery, thus keeping to the traditional five parts. A study of the analyses proposed by Bary shows that they are drawn from the same models—mainly Cicero and Quintilian—as those of Le Gras but they are sketchier. The aims (*persuader, émouvoir, plaire*), the types of oratory, the parts of the *harangue*, the treatment under elocution of words, phrases, figures, periods—all the usual furniture is there, but the effect as a whole seems less tidy. Bary does manage an occasional touch of humor, which gives some relief from the steady and solemn enthusiasm shown by Le Gras for his subject. Bary has a feeling for the possibilities of irony in long enumerations. The orator must be, he says, inventive, learned, judicious, intelligible, diligent, virtuous, observant, and careful of his pronunciation. In commenting on the second of these qualities, he builds up a period that is not without malice:

> Si la rhétorique est vague et indéterminée; si tout ce qui peut tomber sous la connaissance, peut servir de matière à l'oraison, si l'on ne dispose des auditeurs, que par la multiplicité des raisons et des expériences, des exemples et des autorités; si l'on ne triomphe des esprits, que par la connaissance des inclinations et des intérêts, des moeurs et des mouvements: il ne sera pas difficile de faire voir que l'orateur doit entendre la logique et la métaphysique, la physique et la morale, la politique et la jurisprudence, et que celui qui est dépourvu des ces disciplines doit incomparablement plus exercer ses oreilles que sa langue. [Bary, p. 94.]

If we look back at this point to the original problem—to create a rhetoric for the French language—and try to say what the status of the question was after Bary and with Le Gras, we must conclude that an adequate solution had not been found. Neither theorist had shaken off enough of the weight of tradition. The old conception of the *scientia bene dicendi* persisted, with most of its roots in political and legal situations still visible. Both of them adopted with slight change the original plan of the discipline, its chain of actions or processes, starting with invention and ending with delivery. There is a tendency in both to abridge the last two, *memoria* and *actio*. They are working to cut the art loose from its oratorical context so that it may become a more generalized science of expression. This shortening of rhetoric, especially noticeable in Bary, seems more significant than his and Le Gras' efforts to locate the genius and secrets of the French language insofar as they are relevant to persuasive discourse. Although they claim to be doing something new, what they discuss under these topics is usually a reprise in a more systematic framework of things Vaugelas had said in his *Remarques*. The real novelty lies in the effort, sometimes conscious, sometimes not, to get away from formal oratory to an art that is less confined and specific, one that extends without pedantry to the whole field of belles-lettres and not merely to the set speech. The realization of this effort is the achievement of Rapin. And it may thus be said that the French rhetoric of which the Academy projects spoke did not come into being until Rapin really rethought the problems involved in taking language as a basic element in every one of the main artistic and intellectual genres.

1. Pellisson and d'Olivet, *Histoire de l'Académie française* (3rd ed.; Paris, 1743), I, 41. Volume I, written by Pellisson (1624–93), covers the period from the establishment of the Academy until 1652.

2. *Ibid.*, p. 35 (italics Pellisson's).

3. *Ibid.*, p. 132.

4. It will be recalled that even in the case of the dictionary project the Academy had no monopoly: two important dictionaries, those of Richelet and Furetière, appeared in 1680 and 1690, respectively.

5. The assumption being that anyone who tries to write has the prior *sine qua non* of natural gift.

6. *Remarques sur la langue françoise utiles à ceux qui veulent bien parler et bien écrire*, facsimile edition by Jeanne Streicher (Paris, 1934), Préface, p. 3, II.

7. He was, in fact, the original holder of the thirty-second *fauteuil*; and it is known that he was one of the members who took special responsibility in the work on the dictionary.

8. See the *Oeuvres diverses de Mr Patru, de l'Académie française* (3rd ed.; Paris, 1714). In the "Eloge" one reads: "M. de Vaugelas tira de lui de très grands secours pour son excellent livre de *Remarques*, et cet illustre grammairien à qui notre langue est si obligée, confessait devoir à M. Patru les principaux secrets de son art."

9. *Histoire*, II, 166.

10. The discourse he gave when he was received into the Academy so impressed the members that they decided to make such a speech part of the ritual of admission to their company thereafter.

11. See Volume I, page 8, of the "Grands Ecrivains de la France" edition of the works of La Fontaine.

12. *Ibid.*, p. 180. Incidentally, on one occasion, when Patru needed money, Boileau bought his library with the condition that Patru would continue to have the use of it.

13. *Oeuvres*, p. 583.

14. I have used for Bary the revised edition of 1673, published in Paris; for Le Gras, the first edition, also published in Paris. The latter's subtitle reads: " . . . les préceptes de l'ancienne et vraie éloquence: accommodés à l'usage des conversations et de la société civile, du barreau et de la chaire."

15. Pp. [xxx-xxxi].

16. P. [ix]. Le Gras appears not to have known that it was to Patru that Vaugelas referred in his Preface.

17. P. [iv] of the "Discours préliminaire."

18. P. [ii] of the Epître.

19. ". . . Ces deux parties qui donnent aujourd'hui tant de peine aux bons et aux mauvais écrivains. . . . "—Préface, p. i.

20. See *De institutione oratoria* IX. iv. 22.

Chapter II

Problem and Solutions (II)

RHETORIC achieves a new status and a new kind of coherence at the hands of René Rapin. In his *Comparaisons des grands hommes de l'antiquité, qui ont le plus excellé dans les belles-lettres* and in the logical sequel to that work, his *Réflexions sur l'éloquence, la poétique, l'histoire et la philosophie, avec le jugement qu'on doit faire des auteurs qui se sont signalés dans ces quatre parties des belles lettres,*[1] he is not merely translating and paraphrasing his sources. Those procedures would lead one to neglect the differences between the seventeenth century and the times of Aristotle and Cicero. Instead he is rethinking the whole subject in a way that reflects consciously the taste of his contemporaries, consciously though not slavishly, since he aims by his treatises to improve their taste. I believe that his distinctive contribution can be outlined as follows. (1) Whereas the tendency in his ancient sources is to attribute art to the orator alone, Rapin thinks of writer and reader as sharing the same set of qualifications. (2) To an extent and with a degree of rigor not found in his contemporaries, he gathers under a single discipline, based on eloquence, all works of belles-lettres, all modes of expression: eloquence, poetry, history, and philosophy. (3) He modifies the aims of writers and speakers; for him they seek less to persuade us, in the strongly practical sense that the word had in the ancient rhetorics, than to please, instruct, and move us, that is, to affect us in a broader, freer way.

With these generalities in mind, let us look at the structure of Rapin's work. It is a series of eight volumes, divided into four volumes of comparisons (Demosthenes and Cicero, Homer and Virgil, Thucydides and Livy, Plato and Aristotle) and four volumes of reflections (on rhetoric, poetry, history, and philosophy). In spite of what he says at first, that the work is a " . . . recueil de huit volumes, sur toutes les matières principales qui regardent les belles lettres, tous composés les uns après les autres, sans aucun rapport particulier entre eux,"[2] there is an obvious parallelism in the two sets of four volumes. When Rapin begins, after the *coquetterie* of the opening sentence, really to discuss what he has done, he reveals the plan which has been his guide. He presents a number of testimonials to the value of cultivating belles-lettres and then continues:

> Voilà quels étaient les sentiments de ces grands hommes sur le sujet de ces sciences, dont je fais ici l'abrégé: voilà l'estime qu'ils en faisaient. Et j'espère qu'on me saura gré du recueil que j'en donne, pour apprendre à notre siècle une nouvelle manière d'enseigner ces sciences; par l'autorité, en lui proposant de grands exemples; et par la raison, en lui donnant les plus belles maximes qu'on puisse donner, pour un dessein si important. [*Comparaisons*, I, iv–v].

Now this new way of teaching the disciplines in question —by authority and by reason—is an instance of the theological mind at work (Rapin was a Jesuit father) moving into the realm of literature and relating the old distinction of *example/precept* to two ideas usually applied elsewhere, as when one appeals to authority as a certifying principle based on revelation or to reason as a similar principle based on evidence. But this transfer of terms is not the important thing.

We must see what happens to the art of eloquence when one approaches it as an ensemble of examples and maxims. In a sense, it regresses. It loses its technicality and thus it becomes less of a *scientia*. For, strictly speaking, an art or science comes into being at the end of a process involving at least three steps: experiences, reflections on experiences, and the articulation of reflections into a body of knowledge. In other words, in words more appropriate to a productive discipline, knowledge progresses from example to precept to art or method. This last stage is being relaxed by Rapin—not completely abandoned, but made less rigorous. However, what appears to be a serious weakness from the formal point of view of method or inquiry shows itself in another light as a source of strength. One may even say that the vitality of rhetoric in the latter half of the seventeenth century depended on this formal regression. The ancient theories were designed as professional training for specialists who would eventually conceal rather than reveal their technique, in harmony with the principle of *ars celare artem*. Such discipline is obviously too elaborate for a situation in which the audience considers itself as "professional" as the artist, in which poets and those who judge their works share in knowledge of the basic modes of expression. If everyone who matters is interested in eloquence and has or wants to have taste in what concerns it, the technicalities of Aristotle or Quintilian or even of Cicero are out of the question. The same principle applies to the other fields of belles-lettres. They, too, are made more available and less academic by this "nouvelle manière d'enseigner ces sciences," which moves back from their more highly conceptualized and coherent states to the particulars and maxims where they originate.[3]

I have just mentioned Cicero. In the *Réflexions sur l'élo-quence*,[4] Rapin gives him far more space and praise than any other ancient authority. Evidently Cicero's way of treating the art corresponds closely to what Rapin intends.

Cicéron dans les traités qu'il nous a laissés de l'éloquence, n'est pas tout à fait si méthodique qu'Aristote: mais il est plus poli et plus élégant: qui est son caractère essentiel dont il ne se défait jamais. Mais tout solide qu'il est, il n'est pas toujours le plus régulier du monde: parce qu'il pense plus à plaire qu'à instruire.[5]

Cicero has an order, but it is concealed; perfect regularity is for the *savants* only. Cicero's tact in expounding the rules leads Rapin to conclude that " . . . il n'y a point d'auteur, d'où l'on puisse tirer tant de fruit, tant de politesse, tant d'éloquence, tant de solidité, et tant de bon sens que de Cicéron" (*Réflexions*, II, iii). Rapin admires very much the performance of Antonius in the *De oratore*, as he explains with a light touch the rhetors' precepts and as he speaks of questions at law. These are for Rapin the driest of subjects, but Antonius manages to treat them "agréablement et en homme de qualité" (*Réflexions*, II, v).

The praise of Cicero's elegance and lack of pedantry points to something important in Rapin's theory. It leads us, within the broad framework furnished by the notions of "comparisons" and "reflections," to another, more specific tendency in his attempt to reformulate rhetoric. He will try nothing so extreme as replacing it by another discipline: that is the solution of the Port-Royalists, as we shall see. But he is definitely prepared to give more weight to the natural bases of art and to assert the priority of genius in belles-lettres.

Mais après tout, il faut avouer la vérité, quelque avantage qu'on ait en l'éloquence par les instructions de si grands maîtres, l'art y fait moins que le génie: et la plus grande partie des sujets que traite l'orateur sont de telle nature que l'opinion y a plus de part, et a beaucoup plus d'effet que la science . . . et il se trouve des gens dans toutes les professions qui ont de l'éloquence et qui parlent bien, sans en avoir appris aucunes règles.[6]

The usual statement follows to the effect that *both* art and nature must be there for the sake of perfection; still, the theorist is never to be allowed to forget that theory is not indispensable.

Rapin appeals in so many different places to "nature" and to the "natural" that it is not easy, in fact it would be wrong, to assign a fixed value to the term. Nature refers in general to any set of defining characteristics; it is always a given something that has consequences in fact or in reasoning; it is something to argue from, to work from. Each of the main factors in rhetoric—listeners or readers, subjects, and speakers or writers—has a nature in this sense. Taken together these natures form the prior conditions of speech (whether it takes the form of a poem, an oration, or a work of history or philosophy). Discourse is a variable depending on the limits laid down by the other three factors; what to say can never be known until the intelligible aspects of the rest of the situation have been grasped. Subjects may be *grands* and *élevés* or they may be *petits* and *familiers*, according to the natures of the things represented. Listeners are diverse in many ways: they vary as to age, sex, status, native ability, education. They have in common, however, minds, hearts, and feelings, that is, a general human nature, and no orator will really succeed without "une connaissance parfaite du coeur humain" (*Réflexions*, II, 23). And an elementary obligation of the speaker is to "know himself," to understand his own *naturel* or talent, so as to avoid forcing it by putting on manners or speech not suitable to it. Discourse results, therefore, from many particular acts of judgment, all of which go to assure its suitability, its "proportion" to what the subjects, speakers, listeners, and other circumstances are. In "Réflexion XII," Rapin shows clearly how he thinks the orator must proceed and how in a typical instance mistakes occur:

> Quand on s'applique à l'étude de l'éloquence, on a souvent coutume de s'y méprendre par les fausses mesures que l'on prend ou avec soi-même, ou avec son sujet, ou avec ceux à qui l'on parle. . . . L'orateur qui a de l'élévation d'esprit, pèche quelquefois par la trop grande complaisance qu'il a de se suivre lui-même: sans se donner le soin de se proportionner à sa matière, ni de se mesurer à la capacité de ceux à qui il parle.[7]

After all this insistence on nature it comes as no surprise that, when he shifts to the subject of expression, Rapin favors the *tour naturel*, the turn which renders things immediately to the mind with the least possible refraction due to human art. Are not things more striking than the images and figures of elocution? As a consequence the true orator makes no effort to display his art, since distortion would result. Nor, for that matter, does he try to conceal it: "La vraie éloquence n'affecte ni de paraître ni de ne paraître pas: elle a ses principes et ses règles, sans y chercher tant de façon: et l'art véritable ne s'amuse jamais à couvrir ni à découvrir trop d'art." (*Réflexions*, II, 17–18). Art neither shows itself nor hides itself; it simply is, almost in the same way that nature is.

In short, the role of art in eloquence is dwindling before our eyes. It makes no difference that all of the familiar terms having to do with the technique of expression appear in these pages: they are ghosts of what they had been. Of course we know that art, as Rapin understands it, has its rules and principles and processes. And we know that he thinks it to be, as it had traditionally been, a strengthening of natural powers by study, practice, and imitation. Nevertheless, a change has taken place. The knowledge involved has lost its technical status as a productive science or method. As for the strengthening of natural gifts, which seems an essential element of anything that calls itself an art, it is fair to say that the capacity to produce has been replaced by something rather different, by an informal sort of logic directed to the inner aspects of things, in other words, by a capacity to judge. I said earlier that, to Rapin's mind, poets, orators, historians, and philosophers, on the one hand, and their readers or audiences, on the other, should come to share a common knowledge. It is now clear that their common possession should be, more than anything else, this power of discernment, this taste.

In the section entitled "Le Dessein de cet ouvrage" that precedes the *Comparaisons* and *Réflexions*, Rapin asserts: "Je commence ce premier tome par l'éloquence, la plus nécessaire des facultés comprises en ces deux volumes; parce qu'elle est propre à tout" (*Comparaisons*, I, p. [v]). If one puts with this principle, namely, that rhetoric underlies the whole field of disciplined expression in words, the fact that he constantly analyzes rhetorical problems in terms of *nature* and *art*, there arises the question of what place these two leading ideas have in poetry, history, and philosophy. What I wish to do now is to fill in briefly the shadings of these notions as they move in and out of the remaining sets of reflections. This is, I think, the best way to show how Rapin managed to achieve a unified and original discussion of belles-lettres.

In what he says of poetry one is immediately struck by the reappearance of words that gravitated about the "nature" and "art" in his rhetoric. He refers again and again to "moeurs," "passions," "bienséance," "agréments," "nombre," "harmonie," "sujet," "expression." And this last term occurs with its usual *cortège* of adjectives: "congrue," "claire," "naturelle," "éclatante," "nombreuse," and their opposites. There is, however, an obvious novelty: Aristotle's *Poetics* moves into the foreground of the discussion. As result, Rapin adds some Aristotelian trimmings to his earlier vocabulary. For example, it is

33

impossible to follow Aristotle without using the concept of literary types or kinds, and here, in the *Réflexions sur la poétique*, epic, tragedy, comedy, and a string of minor genres furnish topics for Rapin and enable him to specify his observations. Sometimes he modifies—consciously or unconsciously —his basic language in an interesting way, as when he uses *sujet* interchangeably with *fable* (that is, plot) or when he applies *moeurs* not only to the dispositions and habits of the audience, as is usual in the theory of rhetoric, but also to those of the people whom poets represent in dramatic or epic poems.

But these resemblances lie on the surface. A deeper analogy to eloquence emerges in the inevitable attempt to define the end of poetry:

> Les uns veulent que la fin de la poésie soit de plaire: que c'est même pour cela qu'elle s'étudie à remuer les passions, dont tous les mouvements sont agréables. . . . Il est vrai que c'est le but que se propose la poésie, que de plaire: mais ce n'est pas le principal. . . . En effet, la poésie étant un art, doit être utile par la qualité de sa nature, et par la subordination essentielle que tout art doit avoir à la politique, dont la fin générale est le bien public. C'est le sentiment d'Aristote et d'Horace son premier interprète. [*Réflexions*, II, 100.]

This breathtaking promotion of Horace (and Rapin is not, of course, the first to suggest it in his century) leads to the conclusion that the principal aim of poetry is to serve, to *profiter*, and to do that in two ways. First, through relaxation, after which the mind may return with a new strength to its usual tasks. Second, through the instruction which it gives man, or, in the more cautious phrase of Rapin, ". . . qu'elle [la poésie] fait profession de donner à l'homme. . . ."

> Car la vertu étant naturellement austère par la contrainte qu'elle impose au coeur en réprimant ses désirs: la morale qui entreprend de régler les mouvements du coeur, par les instructions, doit plaire pour être écouté: à quoi elle ne réussit mieux que par la poésie. [*Réflexions*, II, 101.]

34

What does this mean? It seems to me to mean that the *nature* —that is, the defining trait—of the audience is exactly the same for poetry as for eloquence. In both instances people are to be taught something or to be improved in an agreeable way. When Rapin treats of eloquence, it is self-evident that instruction is involved; and so he emphasizes pleasure, even to the point of saying that rhetoric is *l'art de plaire*. Similarly, it is obvious that the poet aims to please; that much is taken for granted; the emphasis falls, instead, on the need to instruct. In other words, both arts propose to serve the same two ends, but as different species of belles-lettres they have differing problems of balance in achieving them.

The discussion of utility brings us to a new sense and role of nature in poetry. The aim of instruction, although it orients the poet or critic in a general way, must be specified if it is to be of real use. Rapin does this by linking the lessons of poetry to what is represented in the poetic species; he thinks here of nature as subject matter rather than as the determining principle of the audience. Heroic poetry proposes the examples of great virtues and vices, exciting us (in theory at least) to love the one and to avoid the other. Tragic poetry defines and rectifies, again by outstanding examples, the use of the passions by showing us that vice does not go unpunished, and that good fortune may be more apparent than real. Comedy corrects private faults (and through them public lacks) by putting before us a critical image of ordinary life.

All of this is clearly a discussion of *moeurs*, and of those differences in *moeurs* that have consequences for poets. The universal rule to follow, says Rapin, becoming quite specific, is that one must " . . . représenter chaque personne dans son caractère" (*Réflexions*, II, 116), that is, with the appropriate marks of age, rank, desires, and so on. " . . . Horace dans l'endroit de sa poétique, où il distingue les âges pour en faire

35

des portraits, dit que ce n'est que par la représentation des moeurs qu'on se fait écouter au théâtre: car tout y languit, dès que les moeurs n'y sont pas gardées" (*Réflexions*, II, 118). In short, what is here designated by "nature" has been transferred, so to speak, from the column of *audience* (in the treatment of eloquence) to the column of *res* or subject matter (in the treatment of poetry). As we saw, the orator had to understand his audience in order to adjust the presentation of his thesis to it, and he seeks this understanding in a grasp of human nature, especially as it reveals itself in passions and morals. The poet in turn must understand human nature—approached in the same way as patterns or forms of character and feeling—partly, of course, because he too is obliged to take account of the audience, whose approval he hopes to gain, but mainly because he finds in these dispositions and their consequences what he is called upon to portray. They function as his *thesis*.

"Nature" in its third application refers to the initial gift underlying everything the poet does. Rapin takes six of the first seven *réflexions* to stress its importance. He presupposes in the true poet " . . . un grand naturel," "un esprit juste, fertile, pénétrant, solide, universel," "un grand sens," "une grande vivacité." His best example is Homer " . . . qui eut un génie accompli pour la poésie, et aussi l'esprit le plus vaste, le plus sublime, le plus profond, le plus universel qui fut jamais" (*Réflexions*, II 97). This kind of genius is not to be confused with imagination, nor does it have any connection with poetic *fureur*. The orator may be able to make up for its lack by art; not so the poet. And finally, in the first reflection of the series on the various genres, Rapin advises the poet (as he had advised the orator) to consult his strengths, so as not to attempt less or more than he should according to his gift.

Where eloquence is concerned, Rapin tends, as we have seen, to reduce its complications to something simple like good sense or taste. He continues and carries even further this line of thought in speaking of poetry. Again and again he refers to the role of judgment, to the choices that precede immediately the act of writing. The poet must know how to distinguish, as he works with a serious or elevated subject, between what is beautiful and agreeable in nature and what is ugly and unpleasant.

> Car la poésie est un art où tout doit plaire. Et ce n'est pas assez de s'attacher à la nature, qui est rude et désagréable en certains endroits: il faut choisir ce qu'elle a de beau d'avec ce qui ne l'est pas: elle a des grâces cachées en des sujets qu'il faut découvrir. Quel discernement doit avoir le poète, pour faire ce choix et pour rebuter, sans s'y méprendre, l'objet qui ne plaira pas, et retenir celui qui doit plaire. [*Réflexions*, II, 128.]

"Distinguer," "choisir," "découvrir," "discernement"—every one of these indicates the change in emphasis from the art as a whole to the critical moment or act that Rapin takes as its most important and necessary part.

Another passage shows even more clearly the trend toward simplification—and incidentally, the confidence with which Rapin brings rhetoric into poetics.

> Il y a une rhétorique particulière pour la poésie, que les poètes modernes ne connaissent presque point. Cet art consiste à savoir bien précisément ce qu'il faut dire figurément, et ce qu'il faut dire tout simplement; et à bien connaître où il faut de l'ornement et où il n'en faut pas. . . C'est un pur effet du génie, que ce discernement, et que cette rhétorique particulière, qui est propre à la poésie. [*Réflexions*, II, 128-29.]

37

Thus he goes beyond a reduction of art or method to cultivated judgment; he turns it into a natural gift! But he no
doubt expresses what is for him a more typical view when in
an earlier passage, commenting on the need for the poet to
have a "grand sens," he makes the traditional remark about
the relationship between nature and art, substituting judgment, however, for art: "Mais comme le jugement sans génie
est froid et languissant, le génie sans jugement est extravagant
et aveugle" (*Réflexions*, II, 96).

As is clear from the last three quotations, Rapin's notion
of judgment fluctuates between the *habit* of judging and the
act of judging. I think that the latter is especially characteristic of his analysis. In an important passage he sees particular
judgments according to rules of time, place, action, and so on
as capable of being summed up in a single comprehensive
judgment, made in the light of a single comprehensive value:
bienséance. This is the supreme value that every artistic judgment is designed to affirm or deny of poems or parts of poems.
"Sans elle, les autres règles de la poésie sont fausses. . . .
Enfin tout ce qui est contre les règles du temps, des moeurs,
des sentiments, de l'expression, est contraire à la bienséance,
qui est la plus universelle de toutes les règles" (*Réflexions*,
II, 135–36).

As he reflects on poetry, Rapin uses often and without any
sense of crossing boundaries many terms and principles that
have served him already in the reflections on eloquence. Sometimes he changes the emphases, as in the treatment of enter-
tainment and instruction; sometimes he adds new elements, as
in the case of generic and poetic vocabulary borrowed from
Aristotle. But the bases remain the same. This is especially
noticeable in Rapin's way of transposing the fundamental
themes of nature and art. The "nature" of the reader or
spectator is the same in poetry as in rhetoric (since both poems
and speeches are addressed to someone who is a judge);

however, the term is broadened into human nature as the object which the poet will imitate or represent in his work. The "naturel" of the poet becomes even more decisive than it was before in the case of the orator: here it tends to outweigh all other factors. The movement of art away from elaborate doctrine toward refined judgment, something already clear in Rapin's rhetoric, continues in the discussion of poetry and the introduction of *bienséance* simplifies matters even further. Particular rules are inescapable, since poetry is a form of expression distinct from prose and since it is written in different genres, each of which has its own assumptions and way of coming into being. Nevertheless the many rules that guide the poet's judgment turn out to be based on a single decisive value, appropriateness. To state a rule, to decide a particular point, that is, to make one choice among the indefinitely large number that have to be made in composing a poem, to estimate the worth of a poem as a whole, or even to distinguish from among ancient and modern works those really fit to be admired—any of these acts involves ultimately a reference to *bienséance*.

Rapin takes some pains to distinguish—though with mixed success, as we shall see—his historian from his poet, his orator, and his novelist. One of the first of his reflections on history begins:

> Le roman ne pense qu'à plaire; et l'histoire ne pense qu'à instruire. Voilà proprement leur différence essentielle; celle-ci n'ayant d'autre but à se proposer, que l'instruction du public. Car comme elle ne travaille pas seulement pour le présent, sa vue ne doit pas se borner au temps qui est passager; mais à la postérité, qui dure toujours. [*Réflexions*, II, 220.]

Plaire and *instruire* again: as the aims of literary expression they are never far from the surface of Rapin's mind. In eloquence and in poetry, he believes in a combination of the two. Here he apparently intends to eliminate pleasure as a proper aim for the historian and to assign it to the art of the novelist. But the deeper exigencies of his position soon show themselves. Near the end of this reflection he quotes Thucydides: "J'aime mieux, disait-il, plaire en disant la vérité, que de réjouir en contant des fables" (*Réflexions*, II, 221). And in the marginal heading for the next reflection we read: "Que la vérité est le seul moyen par où l'histoire plaît et va à sa fin." Fiction may please, but so also may the truth; and so, once more, Rapin can suggest that the writer seek two aims simultaneously.

As a matter of fact the image of the austere reader delighting in truth changes soon after. Rapin calls him *distrait* and *volage* when he takes up the essential procedure of history, which is narration. He does not dismiss such a reader; far from it: it becomes the business of the historian to keep him reading. One of the great beauties of narration, he continues, resides in skilful transitions, thanks to which the reader moves from subject to subject "sans se lasser" (*Réflexions*, II, 232). And so, although in his initial distinction of the tasks of the novelist and the historian he discards the rule of pleasure for the latter, he later finds himself unable to proceed without it. The story is repeated when Rapin tries to distinguish history from poetry and oratory according to the presence or absence of figurative language. The historians will use figures sparingly to enliven their accounts and to avoid *froideur,* while orators and poets speak mainly and appropriately in such language, poets being especially free to try unusual turns of thought and expression. The closer one looks, the more this difference dwindles to one of degrees. In fact, at one place it reaches the vanishing point, as Rapin quotes from Cicero, "Magnum quid historiam recte scribere et summi oratoris proprium" (*Réflexions*, II, 268).

In the reflections on history we see once more the concern with nature and art, or, more specifically, with audience, work, and author as distinct but interrelated factors. I have already suggested in connection with the aims of the historian how his audience resembles the audience of poetry and eloquence. There are some nuances worth noting, however. Taking his cue, I think, from the beautiful phrase of Thucydides, who intended his history to be a "thing for all time," Rapin endows the readers of historical eloquence with a special dignity.

Il faut donc penser à écrire noblement, quand on se mêle d'écrire l'histoire. Car dès qu'on parle à toute la terre et à tous les siècles, on est revêtu d'un caractère, qui donne de l'autorité pour élever la voix, parce que c'est aux Rois, aux Princes et aux grands de tous les pays et de tous les âges qu'on parle, et qu'on devient en quelque façon le maître et l'instructeur du genre humain. [Réflexions, II, 206.]

In interpreting these lines, one wants to complete the picture by recalling those passages in which the reader appears easily distracted, easily bored. Even so, Rapin obviously seeks here to establish an obligation bearing on the historian because of the nature of his readers, who are high in rank and who include both present and future generations.

The discussion becomes more subtle when Rapin speaks of another "nature," that of the subject matter entering into the historical work.

C'est un champ bien vaste que la matière propre à exercer l'art d'un historien, puisqu'elle s'étend à toutes les actions des hommes, sur la paix, sur la guerre, les conseils, les négociations, les ambassades, les intrigues, et toutes les différentes aventures qui peuvent arriver dans la vie. Cicéron demande deux qualités dans la matière d'une histoire, que ce soient de grandes choses, et qu'elles soient dignes d'être racontées au public. [Réflexions, II, 215.]

The movement of thought is characteristic: first expansive,

underlining the size and variety of the field of human action; then selective, as the historian's judgment separates by Ciceronian criteria the truly memorable and truly instructive actions from all the rest.

Still, something quite complex remains for him to study and recount: since men are involved, the historian must be a *connaisseur* of motives and characters. Otherwise he is merely a "gazetier" who is satisfied to relate events and results without bothering to inquire into their causes. The point made here sounds very like the obligation of the poet—mentioned above—to represent each person "dans son caractère." Rapin contrasts Livy, the most accomplished of them all, he says, and one of the greatest masters of eloquence who ever lived, with Tacitus, much to the advantage of the former, because he respects the natures of people and of ages.

> C'est ainsi qu'il donne aux derniers rois de Rome tout l'orgueil que leur inspirait l'indépendance; qu'il varie l'esprit de la république . . . qu'il distingue chaque âge et chaque siècle, par le génie qui a le plus régné, sans confondre les mouvements différents de ce génie dans les différentes circonstances des temps, lesquels ne se ressemblent point. [*Réflexions*, II, 218.]

Tacitus fails in this sympathetic variation; it is *his* character that explains what he narrates; too shut up in himself, he makes everything resemble everything else.

The same idea—and the same examples—recur in the discussion of *portraits*, which are a great ornament when they are done a propos.

> Mais c'est un coup de maître, que d'attraper cette ressemblance, laquelle ne consiste que dans les traits singuliers et imperceptibles, qui seuls expriment la nature, et qu'on ne trouve point, à moins de fouiller dans les coeurs, et d'en développer tous les replis, pour faire bien connaître ce qui est caché. [*Réflexions*, II, 251.]

Nature emerges thus at the springs of the actions to be told in history. But it presides likewise over the discussion of the historian's genius.

Rapin began, as we saw, by making him the *maître et instructeur du genre humain,* the chief justice, so to speak, in the court of humanity.

> . . . L'historien est de tous les auteurs celui qui se fait un plan plus vaste, et qui s'érige un plus grand tribunal. Car c'est à juger souverainement de tout ce qui se passe dans le monde, à faire la destinée des grands de la terre, pour leur réputation dans la postérité, et à donner des leçons à tous les peuples pour leur instruction. . . . Car que peut-on imaginer de plus beau que l'histoire, qui sait rendre justice au mérite, et à la vertu, en éternisant les actions vertueuses. [*Réflexions,* II, 205.]

Such evaluative judgment is, I think, a species of something broader and more fundamental: judgment as discrimination. The initial act of the historian as he chooses his subject, the criticism of sources and documents, the conduct of the narration, the drawing of portraits, the analysis of motives, the selection of evocative details—in short, the whole sequence of wide-ranging and innumerable acts through which the historian passes—is a sequence of judgments in this generic sense.

> Quel jugement ne faut-il pas pour prendre en tout le bon parti; tourner les choses dans leur bon sens, aller toujours à ce qui est le plus solide; interposer son sentiment sur les matières dont on parle, sans forcer le lecteur par des préjugés: ne toucher aux endroits délicats, qu'avec cette délicatesse d'esprit qui ne peut être l'effet que d'un sens exquis; ne point charger son discours de trop de matière, qui en étouffe l'esprit, sans y donner place à quelque réflexion qu'on fasse soi-même, ou qu'on donne lieu de faire à son lecteur; savoir trouver le véritable noeud qu'il y a dans chaque affaire sans s'y méprendre, pour l'éclaircir, et en faire le dénouement, ne point débiter de grands événements sur des motifs frivoles; ne point cacher des pensées fausses sous une expression éclatante; éviter ce qui sent l'étude et tout ce qui a l'air contraint, et suivre en toutes choses ce rayon de lumière

43

et d'intelligence qui donne idée du discernement de l'historien, en donnant bonne opinion de sa capacité et de sa suffisance? De sorte que la partie la plus nécessaire à l'histoire est le jugement. [*Réflexions*, II, 269–70.]

As Rapin discusses in this impressive way the *nature* of historical judgment, is he not at the same time defining the sense of *art* (or what is left of it) in history? At every moment of the process, to a degree not required of the orator or the poet, the power of judgment must be aimed at a grasp of the *truth* and of the *true-seeming*. Hence the general warnings in other passages against figures and other stylistic ornaments and the recommendation that one limit oneself to writing *noblement, sensément, purement, simplement*. As with poetry and eloquence, a multitude of particular "rules" and bits of advice is indeed offered concerning narrations, transitions, portraits, passions, descriptions, *harangues*, reflections, and so on, but the complexities of art are frequently telescoped and all arguments referred to the single principle of judgment, to something that is more a matter of psychology or nature than of technique.

Normally the forms of oratory, poetry, and history are immediately accessible to the public, at least to the cultivated part of it. Philosophy usually requires some rewriting for the general reader. Rapin is very conscious of this problem as he undertakes his reflections on philosophy. Luckily he has an ancient model, Cicero (incidentally, a distinguished *rhetorician*).

Je ne suis entré dans aucune discussion des préceptes, qui se débitent dans l'école, pour ne pas languir: je ne m'arrête qu'aux maximes générales, sans rien approfondir. En quoi j'ai tâché d'imiter Cicéron, qui dans ses livres de philosophie ne s'engage presqu'à aucun détail des opinions dont il parle, qu'autant qu'il le peut faire sans rien perdre de sa politesse ordinaire. [*Réflexions*, II, 292–93.]

Cicero explains only the general principles and maxims of each school, adding a few reflections of his own. That is what I have done, says Rapin: "C'est ce que j'ai fait pour m'accorder au goût du siècle, où l'on est moins touché de la grande érudition que du bon sens" (*Réflexions*, II, 293). What this means is obvious: the usual domination of the scene by public tastes and lights. As I have shown, in this theory the reader's judgment in grading a speech or a poem or a history is at bottom equal to that of the one who created the work. What happens when such a reader turns to philosophy as taught by Rapin? "Et comme on trouvera dans le fond de ces réflexions une satire de la fausse philosophie et un éloge de la vraie: je suis sûr par là de plaire à la plus considérable secte des philosophes, qui est celle des honnêtes gens" (*Réflexions*, II, 293). So the answer to the question is that Rapin promotes his reader to the rank of philosopher, and, in fact, gives him an advantage, since the company of *honnêtes gens* is larger than that of the original thinkers. The principles that these thinkers made convincing by putting them into systematic arguments are extracted and made relevant to *savoir vivre*, the really serious philosophical business. We recognize once more the dual aim of instructing and pleasing. But, as I indicated above, there is a significant variation. Rapin had not, after all, felt obliged to restate what Demosthenes and Homer and Thucydides had said. The works of philosophers, however, cannot be absorbed *as they are;* they have to be cut and rephrased lest they repel and in order that philosophical principles or maxims may have some bearing on particular lives. It is clear that in some unspecified balance, Rapin sees such application as more important than pedantic respect for original contexts and intentions.

The love of wisdom, the study of virtue—these are the fundamental qualities of the philosopher, according to Rapin, and the one who possesses them becomes an authority, an example, or even an oracle. Socrates is the philosopher *par excellence.* He had "facilité du génie," "agréments d'esprit," "profondeur," "solidité," "sublimité de lumière et d'intelligence," "simplicité." At other moments, when Rapin has in mind especially the would-be philosopher rather than his ideal, he stresses balance and moderation as characteristics of the philosopher's mind. But I do not think that these traits, however real they may be to him, are as truly basic as something indicated by the term *secte,* used above, and its correlative, *sectateurs,* used elsewhere. By implication these words define the philosopher as the holder of an opinion who has attracted to himself a group of partisans, of people who share his opinion. In other words, Rapin is led by his principles to think of philosophizing, viewed historically, as a kind of rhetorical activity.

Let me be more specific. A Greek philosopher, in his time and setting—so to speak—expounded his views to his friends or to associates in his school; eventually this group came to include thinkers of other ages, and formed " . . . la secte de Socrate, de Platon, des Pyrrhoniens et des Sceptiques, qui est originairement la même" or " . . . celle d'Aristote et des Péripatéticiens" (*Réflexions,* II, 292). As a matter of fact, there were many more schools than these. Rapin confesses that his greatest problem in composing his reflections on philosophy was bringing some order out of this abundance. In his opinion, Plutarch and Diogenes Laertius failed to make any proper distinctions among the sects; Varro counted two hundred and eighty of them; Themistius went as far as three hundred. Rapin contents himself with treatments of the seven "principal" ones and their leaders.

What he goes on to do here, it seems to me, is to bring these *chefs de secte* to a point at which they can communicate with the seventeenth-century audience of "honnêtes gens," that is, with people who belong, after all, to the most considerable group of philosophers. In other words, the scheme is the same, whether he writes the history of philosophy or whether he summarizes it for the use of his readers: a philosopher is a lover of truth and virtue who addresses himself to hearers or readers who have the privilege of agreeing or disagreeing and of determining thus the value of the man, of his speculation, and of his school.

Given such a man, what is the nature of his discourse, or, since in philosophy language and style are less important than content (once obscurities have been removed by clever exposition), what is the subject matter that he studies? Rapin answers in a completely traditional way. The philosopher studies thought itself and its laws in logic; man's desires and the regulation of them in morality or ethics; the world (that is, the entire order of natural and observable things) in physics; and finally, in metaphysics, purely intellectual objects, abstract and spiritual beings. After reflections on philosophy in general—essentially a series of paragraphs commenting on the opinions and historical fortunes of the "sectes"—he offers chapters on each of the four subject matters I have just mentioned.

Now philosophy is not studied for itself alone, but as a way to *savoir vivre*, to a habit of adapting oneself to circumstances and of doing so without loss of one's independence.

A la vérité la plus belle de toutes les philosophies est de savoir vivre: c'est à dire de s'accommoder aux temps, aux personnes, aux affaires, quand la raison le demande: mais cela même doit se faire librement et sans contrainte; pour ne pas imiter ces âmes faibles, qui n'ont que des sentiments empruntés sur chaque chose, et qui s'abaissent à avoir de la condescendance pour des opinions auxquelles ils ont peine à se soumettre: parce qu'ils n'ont pas la force de garder leur liberté entière. [*Réflexions*, II, 343–44.]

47

Since the aim of "la plus belle des philosophies" is unmistakably practical, the study or reading of philosophy is naturally drawn into the status of means to that end. The *savoir* in question comes from reason in its role as judge, as maker of distinctions according to circumstances. One thinks at once of the quality of *bienséance* that Rapin developed so fully in his first two groups of *réflexions*. Eloquence and poetry sought, ultimately, *bienséance* in expression: now philosophy becomes the art of attaining it in action.

The lines quoted show, of course, where the objectives of the "professional" philosopher lie, but they also serve to define the attitude and posture, that is, the *nature,* of his audience. They point to a definite expectation on the part of *honnêtes gens* who read philosophy or reflections on it. Furthermore, although the present passage makes no mention of religion, there are many others that leave no room for doubt: *savoir vivre* means knowing how to live as a Christian. This one for example:

> Ainsi, pour ne pas nous méprendre, commençons à étudier ce qu'il faut croire, avant que de penser à raisonner. Réglons l'usage de notre foi, pour régler l'usage de notre raison; soyons Chrétiens avant que d'être philosophes; que notre première sagesse et notre principale philosophie soit notre religion. [*Réflexions*, II, 423.]

Such are the practical and religious dispositions that characterize the audience in this epiphany of the familiar rhetorical triad—and this piece of the picture matches the other two. One sees the congruence of the parts in a scheme that makes of the philosopher an advocate, of philosophy a position reducible to maxims or opinions, and of the reader or hearer someone who distinguishes the true from the false and the useful from the harmful in view of natural and Christian ends.

48

In philosophy Rapin finds it easy, from one point of view, to identify the appropriate *art*: it is logic. But in his reflections on logic he tends regularly to generalize, to avoid a systematic presentation in favor of examples and anecdotes. Once more the controlling notion of judgment comes to the foreground, although it is true that he develops the theme according to some new values. In the first place, one must pay attention to the different degrees of certainty that are attained in judgments. "C'est une grande science de juger des choses selon les différents degrés de certitude qu'elles peuvent avoir, de démêler la vérité des apparences; de prendre pour opinion ce qui n'est qu'opinion, et de savoir bien distinguer ces jugements pour juger sainement de tout" (*Réflexions,* II, 331). This suggests an art of judging that is focussed on particular propositions and on the modes according to which predicates are said of subjects. In other places Rapin emphasizes the interrelationships of judgments: they may be balanced against each other as opposed extremes or one judgment may stand as a mean between extremes.

For example, he advises us to stay in the *voies ordinaires* (*Réflexions,* II, 332); as soon as one leaves these paths and rejects widely shared opinions or sentiments, one runs the risk of falling into absurdity. Or again, he notes a difference between "esprits" that are naturally free and masterful and those who are "naturellement esclaves" (*Réflexions,* II, 335); he thinks both are extremes. In another instance, he criticizes equally those who never have any doubts and those who are doubtful of everything; the proud man who will not approve of anything for fear of submitting to something and the "volage" who approves of everything in order to spare himself the effort required to do some thinking of his own. "S'accommoder de tout et ne s'accommoder de rien, ce sont d'autres extrémités à éviter à un sage" (*Réflexions,* II, 340).

49

And so the most accessible kind of regulation for judgment here would seem to come to these two pieces of advice: (1) in judging, distinguish, of course, the true from the false, but also note degrees of certainty within the category of truth; and (2) avoid extremes. Logic as the *art* of thinking in philosophy becomes some such technique of balanced discrimination.

In its ancient forms, as well as in its later derivations or counterparts, rhetoric is in essence a discipline that regulates transactions involving words in which what is said is part of an effort to secure the adherence of a listener or a reader to the views of a speaker or writer. One may, therefore, isolate in the rhetorical situation four aspects or dimensions—speaker, audience, speech, and aim—three of which I have just analyzed as they appear in the *Réflexions* of Rapin. The custom of Aristotle, Cicero, and Quintilian is to specify the audience according to the kind of occasion for decision: deliberative (concerning what should be done); judicial (concerning what has been done); or epideictic (concerning the quality of a thing or a person). A particular set of circumstances leads to words addressed to people who then make up their minds, with consequences for that situation. In at least two of these cases (my reservation applies to the "judicial" category), the audience is heterogeneous and is characterized by a wide range of notions and feelings that enter directly into the orator's calculations. In Rapin's theory, the conception of the audience moves definitely in the direction of a homogeneous elite, *les honnêtes gens,* who have culture, standing, and, in some cases, money for patronage.

Having narrowed considerably the focus of rhetoric as regards the composition of the audience, Rapin goes on to broaden the traditional notion of rhetorical occasions or circumstances. Set pieces of public oratory belong to his subject matter, of course, but so does any instance of disciplined speech, no matter where it falls: in eloquence proper, in poetry, in history, or in philosophy. This broadening does not come as something invented suddenly and wholly by Rapin. In many critical works of smaller compass, it had already left its effect on the vocabulary used in discussing works other than orations. The fundamental rhetorical processes of invention and expression, which are by nature hard to pin down, lent themselves to such uses. The feat of Rapin is to gather into a whole *de grande envergure* the principles and consequences of this unsystematized tendency.

By thus extending rhetoric to new fields, Rapin complicates the role of the audience as judge of expression. The place of antilogism, the inevitability of shocks between opposed statements in matters of law or civic policy, had always been recognized in rhetorical theory. But the judge, whether thought of as one person or as an assembly of many persons, was hardly in the wide-open situation of Rapin's reader, who has before him, especially during the process of forming his taste, an immense number of works in a variety of genres.

The change in the audience and in the scope of rhetorical judgment involves a change in the orator: he becomes anyone " . . . qui se mêle d'écrire et de parler." He had been an expert in possession of a genuine science that made him the master of the rhetorical situation. In Rapin's analysis this productive virtue, with its content of clear and certain knowledge, is redefined as a habit of judgment. It is based on experience that may in turn give rise to reflections or maxims (when it bothers to make itself explicit) rather than to organized theory. It is more immediate than discursive in its way of working; and at times it seems less a habit than a natural power.

In the most radical change of all, perhaps, the writer or speaker now faces judges who equal him in understanding, background, and taste. I say *faces;* this is actually the expression of an ideal; Rapin looks forward to a time when poets, orators, historians, and philosophers, on the one hand, and their audiences, on the other, will all recognize essentially the same rules and act according to essentially the same taste. If anything, Rapin wants to do more for audiences than for authors:

> Je ne dirai rien de l'excellence et du prix de ces lettres, sans lesquelles la vie ne peut presque avoir aucune douceur ni aucun agrément pour un honnête homme: parce que l'on trouve dans le commerce de ces sciences tous les plaisirs de l'âme et tous les cette honnêteté qui fait le commerce le plus doux de la vie, que l'on ne peut parvenir presque à aucun degré de politesse, ni de cette honnêteté qui fait le commerce le plus doux de la vie, que par quelque teinture de ces facultés et par quelque connaissance de ceux qui y ont excellé. [*Comparaisons,* I, (iii–iv).]

But this *honnête homme,* this enlightened consumer (to speak as Valéry might), is on the way to becoming, as he approaches his ideal, a producer as well. Rapin continues:

> Ce ne fut que par là que Mécénas devint le favori du plus grand empereur du monde, et le plus honnête homme de la cour la plus polie qui ait peut-être jamais été. Outre qu'il avait un discernement exquis pour tous les ouvrages de l'esprit, il en faisait lui–même: et il encourageait ceux qui avaient du génie pour les lettres, encore plus par son exemple que par ses liberalités: car il faisait de beaux vers. [*Comparaisons,* I, (iv).]

It would not be possible, I think, to say more clearly what Rapin has done to Quintilian: his teaching ideally forms, not the cultivated orator-statesman, but the courtier-connaisseur-patron who writes verse *à ses heures.*

In his Cicero and his Quintilian, Rapin read that the end of rhetoric is persuasion by means of discourse that pleases, instructs, and moves. It seems to be true that means tend naturally to substitute themselves for ends; in any case, that happens here. For one thing, persuasion refers to something too specific for a scheme as broad as this one, which includes all the divisions and subdivisions of belles-lettres; for another, the term has essentially practical connotations: it suggests an agreement followed by action. Obviously Rapin needed a more flexible and speculative end. He found the answer in what had been the means to persuasion, in *delectare, docere,* and *movere.* Eloquence, he writes, is the "véritable art de plaire"—and at one stroke he has left behind all that limited him in persuasion. But note also the rest of the sentence: "L'éloquence, qui est le véritable art de plaire, n'y réussit jamais mieux qu'en imitant la nature." [8] This satisfies the instructive function, while subordinating it as a means to pleasure. (I interpret *nature* here as any object or person which furnishes, when imitated by an author and recognized by his public, the speculative value I have just mentioned.) Rapin does not forget *movere:*

> L'éloquence qui ne touche que l'esprit, et ne va pas jusques au coeur, n'est pas une véritable éloquence. . . . Et s'insinuant par des voies imperceptibles dans l'âme de ceux à qui elle parle, elle fait sur eux de si puissantes impressions, qu'ils semblent agir moins par jugement et par conseil, que par l'émotion et par impétuosité. Ainsi toutes ces beautés qui vont à l'esprit sans aller au coeur, ne sont point de véritables beautés. . . . [*Réflexions,* II, 20.]

Above all the work must please, and the way to that end lies in appeals to thought and to feeling, in that order. In other words Rapin modifies and realigns the traditional principles: the over-riding aim of *persuadere* tends to disappear into *docere* and that plus *movere* become the means to *delectare.*

The Academy had agreed on its prospectus in 1635. In 1684, Rapin published the complete set of his *Comparaisons*

and *Réflexions.*[9] What had been a live problem for almost
fifty years had at last found its solution. A synthesis of considerable power, backed by erudition tactfully used, it was
far superior to anything his immediate predecessors had done.
Vaugelas had stopped short of the main job, leaving it for
Patru; Patru had lived and talked rhetoric but had not
written it down; Bary and Le Gras had for the most part
copied and rephrased Quintilian, since they understood the
problem as a call to import ancient theory into the seventeenth century. Rapin saw that the old had to be thought
through again, that it must be recast in an attractive form if
it was to become truly available. He continues a conservative
and backward-looking tradition but he shows signs of a genu-
inely independent talent: in the unusual structure of the
work, in its steady effort to be discriminating, in its accessibility, in its style. Contrary to the expectations of the Academy, the composition of a French rhetoric did not precede
the writing of great literary works. Practice and the development of theory went hand in hand, each explaining or illustrating the other; and when Rapin's synthesis appeared in
its final form, French classicism was over. For us the special
value of his work comes from this vital interrelation. I know
of no better contemporary source to which one may turn
for a summary of the literary culture to which the *honnête
homme* aspired and of the common doctrine that writers knew
even when they chose to interpret it freely.

1. These are the titles of the Paris edition of 1684 in two volumes.
They are repeated in the Amsterdam edition of 1709, also in two volumes,
to which my footnotes refer. Where quotations are drawn from Volume I,
I have identified them by the abbreviation *Comparaisons*; where they are
taken from Volume II, I have used *Réflexions.*

2. From "Le Dessein de cet ouvrage," *Comparaisons*, I, p. [i].

3. Rapin recalls to his readers the story of Marcellus, who, according
to Plutarch, gave Rome the "amour des belles choses" by pictures and

statues that he brought back from Syracuse and showed to the public. "C'est ce que je voudrais tâcher de faire, c'est-à-dire, d'affectionner notre siècle aux belles-lettres en lui proposant les grands modèles. . . . C'est même une espèce de méthode de devenir savant pour les gens de qualité, sans les obliger à descendre dans un détail trop mécanique de préceptes, et sans tomber dans les minuties de la construction et de la grammaire, qui est toujours désagréable aux gens d'un esprit déjà avancé" (*Comparaisons*, I, p. [v]). From the point of view of rhetorical theory, it has seemed to me more useful to study here the *Réflexions* rather than the *Comparaisons*. But the latter have a definite place in Rapin's program, as the lines just quoted show clearly.

4. A detailed analysis of these reflections would be out of place here. For the wide scope of Rapin's exposé, note these lines: "Le premier volume qui contient les réflexions sur l'éloquence a trois parties, les réflexions sur l'éloquence en général selon l'usage qu'elle a dans les lieux où l'on parle, sur l'éloquence du barreau, et sur l'éloquence de la chaire. Sur quoi tout ce qui peut s'observer dans l'usage de ces trois sortes d'éloquence est exactement observé: avec toutes les règles que chacun demande par son caractère dans un assez grand détail" (*Comparaisons*, pp. [vii–viii]).

5. Préface, *Réflexions*, pp. [ii–iii].

6. *Ibid.*, p. [viii]. Cf. also: "L'éloquence qui est le véritable art de plaire n'y réussit jamais mieux qu'en imitant la nature: ce n'est pas un moyen fort sûr pour persuader que de donner trop à l'art. . . . Le souverain art de l'éloquence est de s'attacher scrupuleusement à la nature comme à son premier original" (*ibid.*, pp. 16–17).

7. *Ibid.*, p. 13. Other mistakes easily interpretable according to the basic schema are: " . . . De réprésenter les objets plus grands que le naturel; de prendre un grand air en de petites affaires; d'affecter de grandes expressions en de petits sujets; faire le bel esprit avec le peuple; vouloir être ardent et pathétique dans des sujets qui ne le méritent pas; accabler les esprits faibles par des discours trop forts."—*Ibid.*, p. 13. The explanation is always the same. " . . . Dès qu'on sort de la nature, tout devient faux dans l'éloquence" (*ibid.*, p. 17).

8. *Ibid.*, p. 13.

9. He had published them in separate volumes over the period from 1664 to 1681. Here are some salient facts. (1) *Comparaisons*: Homer and Virgil (two French editions in 1664 and 1669; three in Latin in 1684, 1704, and 1707); Demosthenes and Cicero (two editions in 1676); (2) *Réflexions*: on poetics (editions in 1674, 1675, and again in 1675); on eloquence (editions in 1671, 1672, and 1679). The comparison of Plato and Aristotle appeared in 1671, that of Thucydides and Livy in 1681. The reflections on philosophy were published in 1676. I have found no sign of separate publication of the reflections on history; they may be combined in the *Instructions pour l'histoire* of 1677 and 1690, but I have not been able to consult either of those editions. Rapin's *Oeuvres* were published in 1709 and 1725; they included the *Comparaisons* and *Réflexions*. These dates and indications give some idea of the success and continuing impact of Rapin's thought. See also note 1, above, for the reference to the collected edition of the *Comparaisons* and *Réflexions* in 1684.

55

Chapter III

Port-Royal: Logic vs. Rhetoric (I)

T͟HE SECOND EDITION of the *Logique* of Port-Royal, which
appeared in 1664, includes an interesting *discours*. It is the
second of two printed at the beginning of the volume. In
this very substantial essay the authors—Arnauld and Nicole—
undertake to defend their logic against objections aroused by
the first edition of 1662. One of these criticisms takes as its
point of departure that what is supposed to be a treatise on
logic contains so many sallies into rhetoric, ethics, physics,
metaphysics, and geometry. The authors give first a general
answer: in these excursions they can demonstrate the applica-
bility of their precepts. Instead of being an isolated exercise,
logic moves into any and all discussions with its special help
in the arts of knowing and judging. Then comes comment
on several disciplines in particular; and rhetoric leads the list:

> On a considéré, par exemple, en ce qui concerne la rhétorique,
> que le secours qu'on en pouvait tirer pour trouver des pensées,
> des expressions, et des embellissements, n'était pas si considé-
> rable. L'esprit fournit assez de pensées, l'usage donne les expres-
> sions; et pour les figures et les ornements, on n'en a toujours
> que trop.[1]

They refer, thus, immediately to invention and expression,

the principal moments of the rhetorical process, at least in its simplified form in which it concerns not oratory but communication in general; and they lose no time in revealing an attitude toward the art that is basically hostile.

They see no need for a method of invention and expression, since natural facility and usage are already more than sufficient. The addition of art leads one into bad ways of speaking and writing; it encourages false and hyperbolic thoughts, forced figures, and other vices of the "style rhétoricien." [2] The real need is for a restraining force. One should not give free rein to thought in an inventive phase, and then, at the moment of expression, look about for elaborate ways of saying what one has found. Thought is supposed to be adequate to its object, not abundant; words are supposed to be a medium, not an element that attracts attention to itself thanks to decoration. These Jansenist minds know where to locate the restraining force—in their logic: "Or l'on trouvera peut-être autant de choses utiles dans cette logique pour connaître et pour éviter ces défauts que dans les livres qui en traitent expressément" (*Logique*, p. 28).

I think it easy to see the reason for conflict and competition between these two arts. When thought and expression are removed from their full rhetorical and practical context (we have seen an outstanding example of this typical trend in Rapin's theory), there is nothing to separate the art which had traditionally regulated them from *l'art de penser,* the discipline of thought wherever it is exercised, in practice or in theory. The increasing prestige of mathematics and physics had a part in this process of comparison and interference. The partisans of the sciences generalized their techniques and sought new applications for them in a way that reminds one very much of the expansionist tendencies of the rhetoricians. And so, with the Cartesian sureness and consistency that is so remarkable in the *Logique*, Arnauld and Nicole report at the outset on those areas where their art has met and purified rhetoric.

In the last chapter of Part I, for example, they have defined the proper role of the figured style and given the "true rule" for distinguishing the good figures from the bad ones. In the chapter on *lieux*, or commonplaces, they have proposed ways of avoiding the empty *copia* that rhetoricians usually admire. In the chapter on errors in reasoning, they have insisted that the false can never be beautiful:

> L'article où l'on parle des mauvais raisonnements où l'Eloquence engage insensiblement, en apprenant à ne prendre jamais pour beau ce qui est faux, propose en passant une des plus importantes règles de la véritable rhétorique, et qui peut plus que toute autre former l'esprit à une manière d'écrire simple, naturelle et judicieuse. [*Logique*, pp. 28–29.]

As Boileau was to say, eleven years later, "Rien n'est beau que le vrai. . . . " Finally, in this same chapter, they have stressed the care one should take not to irritate those to whom one speaks: one thus avoids " . . . un très grand nombre de défauts d'autant plus dangereux, qu'ils sont difficiles à remarquer" (*Logique*, p. 29). On that point the gentlemen of Port-Royal spoke from experience!

Such are the points where the authors turn explicitly to rhetoric and use on it the astringent power of logic. In reality the implications of what they do are even more radical. The section on method (Part IV), one of the innovations in this logic, contains a latent mine of arguments against eloquence and its devices; and beyond that, the narrow conception of thought itself taken by Arnauld and Nicole as their starting point can never be reconciled, in any real sense of the word, with the liberal notion of elements or factors of persuasion on which the ancients had based their *scientia bene dicendi*.

The first passage relevant to the theory of rhetoric comes in the discussion of the meanings of words. After examining the way words signify, the authors of the *Logique* conclude that words have principal and accessory meanings. They consequently recognize two degrees of expression. The first of these is aimed at when we try, by strict attention to the meanings of words, to utter or write "la vérité toute nue" (*Logique*, p. 128). The second degree is sought when, in addition to telling the truth about things, we wish to convey the emotions we experience in conceiving or speaking of them. Such speech has the curious property of arousing feelings similar to ours in other people: whoever uses the figured style—the technical term for the second degree of expression—will be more moving to his listeners or readers, because the soul, though *instructed* by images of truths, is *affected* mainly by images of feelings ("mouvements"). Arnauld and Nicole quote the inevitable maxim from Horace: "Si vis me flere, dolendum est / Primum ipsi tibi" ("If you wish me to weep, you must first grieve yourself.")

Something of what they mean by *figure* is clear from the example they give, part of a line from Virgil: "Usque adeone mori miserum est?"[3] ("Is it, then, so painful to die?") In other words, the line would have been much less moving had it been merely a declaration, with the words arranged in the normal order for such a case. I infer, therefore, that the turns in question are what are traditionally called figures of thought, as opposed to figures of words or speech. A discussion such as the present one, located in the part of logic that deals with thought, conception, and definition, emphasizes predictably the kind of figurative expression which bears on what is said and on emotion rather than on word patterns as such.

One may use language, then, for the exact rendering of thought or for communicating feelings as well. The problem is to decide when each of these styles is appropriate. As for the "style figuré":

> Il est visible qu'il est ridicule de s'en servir dans les matières purement spéculatives, que l'on regarde d'un oeil tranquille, et qui ne produisent aucun mouvement dans l'esprit. Car puisque les figures expriment les mouvements de notre âme, celles que l'on mêle en des sujets où l'âme ne s'émeut point, sont des mouvements contre la nature, et des espèces de convulsions. [*Logique*, p. 129.]

There is nothing less agreeable than certain sermons where the *prédicateurs* exclaim indifferently about everything and are just as agitated in moments of philosophical reasoning as in what they say of the most striking and necessary truths of salvation. As faults go, improper presence of figures is matched by improper absence of them. Here the Port-Royalists criticize the scholastics for the bareness of their style. Their manner of expression is less capable of arousing feelings of respect and love for Christian truth, and also less agreeable because, for the listener, pleasure comes more from feeling than from pure learning.

The position of the *Logique* is now clear: not elimination of a favorite rhetorical device, but restriction in the use of it, restriction so severe that it calls into question the place of emotion as a persuasive force of which a speaker may avail himself. One may agree with Port-Royal that preaching is an essential activity and still go on to ask what consequences this doctrine of levels of expression will have for the large number of people who are not involved directly in the saving of souls but who do care about method and good judgment in secular affairs. There the problem of using rhetoric as an art of thought and expression (and even of behavior) becomes acute. On good classical precedent it claimed to be a universal technique; in what appears to be merely a brief discussion of figures, Arnauld and Nicole are actually challenging the structure of rhetorical discipline. For they are cutting out, in everything except sacred oratory, most of the third link in the rhetorical chain of invention, arrangement, and elocution. Their attitude represents, in the first place, a tremendous change in emphasis. With the authority of Cicero behind him, Quintilian speaks of elocution as the hardest part of rhetoric: "Plus exigunt laboris et curae quae sequuntur. Hinc enim jam elocutionis rationem tractabimus, partem operis, ut inter omnes oratores convenit, difficillimam." ("More work and diligence are required in what follows. For now we shall discuss the theory of elocution or style, which is the most difficult part of the art, as all orators agree.") (*De institutione oratoria* VIII. proemium. 13.) It is the process in which art shows itself most clearly, invention and arrangement being within the capacity of any intelligent man. "Et Marcus Tullius inventionem quidem ac dispositionem prudentis hominis putat, eloquentiam oratoris, ideoque praecipue circa praecepta partis hujus laboravit." ("Cicero, too, believes that any intelligent man is capable of invention and arrangement, but elocution belongs to the orator alone, and consequently he gave particular care to the rules for this part of the art.") (*Ibid.*, 14.) The real orator comes into his own at this point.

In the next place, the very nature of the expressive process, as viewed by the rhetorician, is bound to conflict with the assumptions and special interests of the logician. The former sees that process as a movement from correctness ("latinitas") to clarity and order ("perspicuitas" and "collocatio") to elegance ("ornatus," "figurae"). Thus Quintilian: "Igitur, quam Graeci φράσιν vocant, latine dicimus elocutionem. Ea spectatur verbis aut singulis aut conjunctis. In singulis intuendum est ut sint latina, perspicua, ornata, ad id quod efficere volumus accommodata; in conjunctis, ut emendata, ut collocata, ut figurata." ("What the Greeks call *phrasis*, we name in Latin elocution or style. It may be considered in individual words or in groups of words. Where they are taken singly, we must be sure that they are Latin, clear, elegant and appropriate to the desired effect; where they are joined together, we must see to it that they are correct, well-placed, and adorned with figures.") (*De institutione oratoria* VIII. i. i.) In other words, in its last and most important stage, expression necessarily tends away from the simple to the complex, from the usual to the rare. The emphasis on tropes and figures, the subtleties, the numerous and overlapping definitions—to the logician all of these are clearly extravagant. To him the art of eloquence serves mainly to complicate gratuitously the problem of expressing and conveying truth.

Finally, in the third place, the Port-Royalists distrust in a basic way the power that obviously lies in speech fashioned by this art. The affirmations of Cicero and Quintilian concerning the admiration for the speaker and the sympathy for his cause which are aroused by rhetorical devices easily seem to ally themselves with duplicity, with insincerity, with willingness to *faire flèche de tout bois*, so long as the end is achieved.[4] *Rien n'est beau que le vrai* as a principle is undermined by any such pragmatism (and I believe that rhetoric is definitely a species of pragmatism); it is in danger of becoming *rien n'est vrai que l'utile,* and beauty need not necessarily belong to or result from a true demonstration, since it is something that has been added to thought.

And so the Port-Royalists solve the problem by distinguishing firmly between the language of *matières purement spéculatives* and discourse on religious matters. Instead of pages and pages of turns and figures of speech and thought, with comments and examples of their power, use, and misuse, we have a short treatment of the way words signify. In addition to their principal references, they have accessory meanings, that is, indexes of feeling. A figurative style, such as one sees in the church fathers and in the practice of those who preach well, may properly work with these accessory meanings.

The extreme reduction worked on the topics of figures and elocution is matched by another and more explicit attack—the word is not too strong—on traditional rhetorical theory. It occurs in chapter XVI of Part 3 of the *Logique* ("Du raisonnement"). The heading of the chapter reads tendentiously, "Des lieux ou de la méthode de trouver des arguments. Combien cette méthode est de peu d'usage" (p. 290). The first thing to note is the point in their treatise at which the Port-Royalists choose to discuss the commonplaces or starting points of rhetorical reasoning. That choice gives right away an idea of the revolution in intellectual style at which the *Logique* aims. In Aristotle, in Cicero, in Quintilian, invention comes first, before all matters of arrangement and expression; in this work Arnauld and Nicole do not approach the subject until they have first considered problems of ideas or conceptions and problems of judgment (that is, of combining ideas), until in fact they have almost reached the end of the treatment of reasoning (that is, of combining judgments). To be precise, we hear nothing of invention until the doctrine of Port–Royal has been expounded in its positive phase and the moment for critical or polemic conclusions is at hand.

The authors know exactly what they are doing; their position strikes directly at a key point of ancient theory: "Il est donc assez inutile de se mettre en peine en quel ordre on doit traiter des lieux, puisque c'est une chose à peu pres indifférente. Mais il serait peut-être plus utile d'examiner s'il ne serait point plus à propos de n'en traiter point du tout" (*Logique*, p. 291). They realize that the ancients had a high esteem for this subject which may be treated in any order and which may indeed be skipped altogether.

> On sait que les Anciens ont fait un grand mystère de cette méthode, et que Cicéron la préfère même à toute la dialectique, telle qu'elle était enseignée par les Stoïciens, parce qu'ils ne parlaient point des lieux. . . . Quintilien et tous les autres rhétoriciens, Aristote et tous les philosophes, en parlent de même; de sorte que l'on aurait peine à n'être pas de leur sentiment, si l'expérience générale n'y paraissait entièrement opposée. [*Logique,* pp. 291–92.]

One winces to see the juxtapositions and mixings made so readily in that passage. In a train of sweeping formulas Cicero, "Quintilien et tous les autres rhétoriciens, Aristote et tous les philosophes . . ." are presented as saying essentially the same things. Arnauld and Nicole do not bother to discriminate between the thorough pedagogy of Quintilian and the urbane discretion of Cicero—but I suppose that that difference is not, after all, a basic one. More striking is that they obviously fail to keep separate what Aristotle said in his theory and what later happened to rhetoric when it was turned into a method applicable everywhere. For Aristotle, rhetoric was one art among many arts and sciences, having its specific purpose (persuasion) and its subject matter (questions not susceptible of a scientific treatment that arise in particular circumstances before a particular audience); whereas for Cicero and Quintilian, it is *the* art, *the* science; in fact, for them it is coextensive with philosophy. It even improves on philosophy by virtue of its technique of expression, which makes wisdom easier to communicate and to practice than would otherwise be possible. These differences in ways of defining the art are not casual but pervasive, so that invention or the use of commonplaces can never refer to the same thing in Aristotle and in the two others.

65

Niceties of historical semantics do not interest the authors of the *Logique*. They have evidently taken as their basic text something like the enthusiastic chapters in Book II of Cicero's *De oratore*. For example, one reads there: "His igitur locis in mente et cogitatione defixis et in omni re ad dicendum posita excitatis, nihil erit quod oratorem effugere possit, non modo in forensibus disceptationibus, sed omnino in ullo genere dicendi." [5] ("With these commonplaces fixed in one's mind and memory and called up with every subject proposed for discussion, there is nothing that can escape the orator, not only in matters debated in the forum, but in any kind of eloquence.") But general experience, the experience of almost all those who have studied the "méthode des lieux" belies this optimistic view. Is there a single one, the authors go on to ask, who learned this technique in the *collèges* and who can really say that, when he came to treat some subject, he reflected on the commonplaces and that he found there the principles he needed? However, there are more fundamental objections, theoretical ones this time, to the use of this method. Here the Port-Royalists turn to St. Augustine:

De sorte que l'on peut dire véritablement des lieux ce que Saint Augustin dit en général des préceptes de la rhétorique. On trouve, dit-il, que les règles de l'éloquence sont observées dans les discours des personnes éloquentes, quoi qu'ils n'y pensent pas en les faisant, soit qu'ils les sachent, soit qu'ils les ignorent. Ils pratiquent ces règles, parce qu'ils sont éloquents; mais ils ne s'en servent pas pour être éloquents. *Implent quippe illa quia sunt eloquentes, non adhibent ut sint eloquentes.* L'on marche naturellement, comme ce même père le remarque en un autre endroit. [*Logique*, p. 293.]

It is the same judgment that they offered in the second preliminary discourse. Natural powers and their operations suffice in knowing and speaking. Nature has no real need of an art to perfect it, and so, as an immediate consequence, rules and commonplaces are denied the fertility that Cicero had seen in them. Instead of helping in a situation where one must find suitable things to say, they merely describe what expert speakers did in the past.[6] Their status is almost, if not entirely, speculative rather than productive. Cicero had objected to the dialectic of the Stoics because it was of no use in finding arguments but limited itself to criticizing and analyzing them once they are found. The Port-Royalists are, in effect, reducing his method of the *loci argumentorum* to the impotence he had hoped to avoid.

Since an inventive art is not necessary, we are not surprised to be told that if we impose and apply one anyway, it may actually hinder and corrupt the operations of the natural powers. The commonplaces, by their very nature, enter into all discourse, " . . . mais ce n'est pas en y faisant une réflexion expresse que l'on produit ces pensées: cette réflexion ne pouvant servir qu'à ralentir la chaleur de l'esprit, et à l'empêcher de trouver les raisons vives et naturelles qui sont les vrais ornements de toutes sortes de discours." [7]

Something even more pernicious, a bad mental disposition, arises from the application of the method. It encourages a facility that is only too common anyway, a readiness to "discourir de tout à perte de vue" (*Logique*, p. 296), and a taste for the *copia rhetorum*; and it discourages willingness to make the effort needed for accurate thought. The Port-Royalists want to lead us away from habits of judgment that depend finally on the audience; the ideal image of people surrendering to the flow of eloquent language has no appeal for them. We should respond instead to the call of the object being known, to the demands of the subject matter. True thought does not invent according to arbitrary recipes; it discovers. The full force of the term "commonplace" is felt here, and that of its antonym, the *proper place*. When one applies a stock of generalities to all objects of inquiry and discussion, distinctions become vague and differences fade into a more or less spurious unity. "L'esprit s'accoutume à cette facilité, et ne fait plus d'effort pour trouver les raisons propres, particulières et naturelles, qui ne se découvrent que dans la considération attentive de son sujet" (*Logique*, p. 295).

Some interesting rapprochements with Descartes suggest themselves here. In the *Discours de la méthode*, his criticisms of scholastic logic and of its concern with the forms of the syllogism take at bottom the same form as those of the Port-Royalists as regards rhetoric and invention. The syllogism, says Descartes, is not a technique for finding the truth, though one may expound what one already knows in that form. The human mind is naturally capable of moving in an orderly fashion from principles to consequences, that is, of deduction. There is no need for it to learn how to go through this process; bringing in at this point a superfluous art, comparable in science to the method of commonplaces in rhetoric, merely invites trouble. Furthermore, the forms of reasoning are dangerous in application because they have a validity that does not depend on the truth of the materials cast in them. They tempt us to let perfection of form legitimize confused ideas and false principles, since the coherence of the argument may make it pass in spite of the content. Descartes, Arnauld, and Nicole obviously share the same confidence in nature[8] and the same desire to set aside formalisms that interfere with the normal workings of human powers. But Descartes is involved also in the trend away from the use of the *lieux communs*. As Gilson points out, Descartes reduces scholastic logic to dialectic, and then dialectic, in turn, to the method of the commonplaces, as is clear from the *Entretien avec Burman*:

Ea potius est dialectica, cum doceat nos de omnibus rebus

disserere, quam logica, quae de omnibus rebus demonstrationes dat. Et sic bonam mentem magis evertit quam adstruit, nam dum nos divertit et digredi facit in hos locos communes et capita, quae rei externa sunt, divertit nos ab ipsa rei natura.[9]

("That is dialectic, when it teaches us to discourse on all matters, rather than logic, which furnishes demonstrations in all matters. And so it overturns good sense instead of building on it; for, as it turns us aside and causes us to digress into commonplaces and topics, which are external to the thing, it diverts us from the nature itself of the thing.")

Ever since Aristotle, rhetoric had been the counterpart in practice of dialectic, and one of the resemblances had been that both disciplines, being divorced from specific subject matters, must appeal for principles to topics or distinctions that are broadly applicable. And now, by a concurrence that underlines once more the deep influence of Cartesianism on Port-Royal, one sees Descartes defending his logic, that is, his method, against dialectic—basically a *theoretical rhetoric* —while Arnauld and Nicole defend essentially the same logic against rhetoric—basically a *practical dialectic*. Each attacks the method of commonplaces wherever he finds it, and for essentially the same reasons.[10]

Between the critical observations on rhetorical topics and the next main section—on method—Arnauld and Nicole insert two chapters on bad reasonings or "sophisms," first in science or theory, and then in civil life and ordinary discourse. The second kind of error concerns us directly, because to uncover certain sophisms is to see through the art of the rhetorician.

Errors of judgment—for here, as always in this logic, the real point of departure is the judgment—are analyzed according to their origins. Some are due to causes within us, in general to abuses of the will, where reasons reflect not the true but the useful or what is advantageous for us. Others arise from the characteristics of things outside us; they deceive us because they *appear* to be, as well as *are*, and we take the appearances for the realities. With necessary cross-references for cases in which a mixing of sources of error occurs, the development follows the two lines indicated by the chapter titles: "Des sophismes d'amour propre, d'intérêt, et de passion" and "Des faux raisonnements qui naissent des objets mêmes."

We do not ordinarily adopt an opinion because of genuine reasons but because of some usefulness it has for us: that is the fundamental fact in this account of false reasoning. It turns almost imperceptibly into an account of how people are effectively persuaded.

> Si l'on examine avec soin ce qui attache ordinairement les hommes plutôt à une opinion qu'à une autre, on trouvera que ce n'est pas la pénétration de la vérité, et la force des raisons; mais quelque lien d'amour propre, d'intérêt ou de passion. C'est le poids qui emporte la balance, et qui nous détermine dans la plupart de nos doutes. . . . Nous jugeons des choses, non par ce qu'elles sont en elles-mêmes; mais par ce qu'elles sont à notre égard: et la vérité et l'utilité ne sont pour nous qu'une même chose. [*Logique,* pp. 333–34.]

Here the Port-Royalists take a characteristic turn. Instead of adjusting themselves to this disturbing personal factor, and exploiting it by the rules of an art, they decry it and *their* rules are designed to reduce or eliminate this factor. To them there is nothing less reasonable than to make our self-interest into a reason for believing something. All that our self-interest can properly do is to lead us to consider more attentively where the truth lies, and " . . . il n'y a que cette vérité, qui se doit trouver dans la chose même, indépendamment de nos désirs, qui nous doive persuader" (*Logique,* pp. 334–35).

Any attempt to teach or persuade another mind must reckon with this pessimistic view of the way persuasion takes place. According to the Jansenists, man is by nature self-centered, he naturally desires every advantage for himself, with the unavoidable corollary that every man is naturally jealous, envious, and ill-disposed whenever he sees some superiority in another. Here is the practical consequence:

> La connaissance de cette disposition maligne et envieuse, qui réside dans le fond du coeur des hommes, nous fait voir qu'une des plus importantes règles qu'on puisse garder, pour n'engager pas dans l'erreur ceux à qui on parle, et ne leur donner point d'éloignement de la vérité qu'on leur veut persuader, est de n'irriter que le moins qu'on peut leur envie et leur jalousie en parlant de soi, et en leur présentant les objets auxquels elle [sic] se puisse attacher. [*Logique*, pp. 340–41.]

The wise man is careful to "se cacher dans la presse" and to hide any marks of personal advantage, lest distaste for his person spread to the opinions he wants to teach. Pascal had carried the rule to its logical conclusion:

> Feu Mr. Pascal, qui savait autant de véritable rhétorique, que personne en ait jamais su, portait cette règle jusqu'à prétendre qu'un honnête homme devait éviter de se nommer, et même de se servir des mots de *je* et de *moi*, et il avait accoutumé de dire sur ce sujet, que la piété chrétienne anéantit le moi humain, et que la civilité humaine le cache et le supprime. [*Logique*, p. 341.]

This fascinating passage shows beyond a doubt the true intention of this section of the *Logique*. If the "genuine kind" of rhetoric tries to do away with all awareness of the speaker, what does that imply for the other kind of rhetoric? The first place to look for an answer, I think, is in the theory of Aristotle. In Book II of his *Rhetoric*, he examines through seventeen chapters the role of the speaker *as a means or source of persuasion* quite apart from his power of inventing arguments. For he takes his place as one of three causes leading to persuasion; the other two are the speech or proof and the dispositions of the hearers.[11] It is essential for the orator to establish early in the game an impression of good sense, good character, and good will (*Rhetoric* II. i. 1378ª. 6). He should, moreover, make the most of the possibility of exciting by knowledge and technique his hearer's feelings. At this point Aristotle enters on his famous and cold–blooded analysis of passions (considering the states of mind in which each is felt, the people toward whom each is felt, and the grounds on which it is felt) and of characters (considering the feelings and qualities that follow typically from various ages and degrees of fortune). He expects the orator to know all these things and to use his knowledge, especially in political oratory and in the law courts, where he will wish to influence juries and audiences by appeals to emotions and to accepted ideas as well as by proofs. Whereas the Port–Royalists see almost exclusively the negative possibilities introduced into the situation by feelings, Aristotle and other ancient theoreticians see both negative and positive possibilities. The emotional factor may work either way; it is, therefore, the business of the art to make this factor serve the advantage of the speaker.

The discussion of πάθος and ἦθος is continued by Cicero and Quintilian, where the analysis becomes even more pragmatic and more sharply focussed on results than it had been in Aristotle. No one of the three functions of the orator (*conciliare, docere, movere*) is sufficient in itself to persuade, though in a particular case one or another of them may need more emphasis. But on the specific point of the need for a speaker to make himself acceptable and amiable to the audience, Antonius speaks with a bluntness that can hardly have escaped the authors of the *Logique*:

. . . Nihil est enim in dicendo, Catule, maius quam ut faveat oratori is qui audiet, utique ipse sic moveatur, ut impetu quodam animi et perturbatione magis quam iudicio aut consilio regatur. Plura enim multo homines iudicant odio aut amore aut cupiditate aut iracundia aut dolore aut laetitia aut spe aut timore aut errore

aut aliqua permotione mentis quam veritate aut praescripto aut
juris norma aliqua aut iudicii formula aut legibus. [*De oratore*
II. xlii. 178.]

("Now in speaking, Catulus, there is nothing more important
than that the hearer be favorably inclined to the speaker and
that he be so moved that he is swayed by some impulse or
excitement of mind more than by judgment or deliberation. For
men decide many more things by hate or love or desire or anger
or grief or joy or hope or fear or error or some other inner
affection than by truth or precept or legal principle or judicial
form or laws.")

So far the diagnosis reads very much like that of the Port-
Royalists: men's opinions depend more on passions than on
truth. However, the orator *accepts* this as a fact and bases on
it his effort to establish a favorable image of himself in the
mind of the listener.

Valet igitur multum ad vincendum probari mores et instituta et
facta et vitam eorum, qui agent causas, et eorum pro quibus, et
item improbari adversariorum animosque eorum, apud quos age-
tur, conciliari quam maxime ad benevolentiam quom erga oratorem tum erga illum, pro quo dicet orator. [*De oratore* II. xliii.
182.]

("It is very important to success that the morals, principles,
deeds, and lives of those who plead cases and of their clients be
approved, and that those of their adversaries be censured; and
also that the minds of the judges be won over as much as possible
to a favorable disposition both toward the speaker and toward
the one on whose behalf he speaks.")

When the topic of *movere* has its turn, we have an even
clearer indication of the lengths to which the advocate will
go in the manipulation of passions for the sake of his case.
It is desirable, says Antonius, that the judge bring to the
case a positive attitude toward the advocate; then the problem
is merely to *currentem incitare*, to spur the galloping horse.
If this starting advantage is lacking, the orator will know how

73

to proceed. Like a doctor studying a patient, he will use all
his energy and thought to grasp the feelings, opinions, and
expectations of the judge, in order to see from what stand-
point he may persuade most easily; he will turn his sail to
the point from which the breeze presents itself. If the judge
has no passions or prejudices, the speaker will have to work
harder, but the power of the word is such that he may work
confidently:

Sin est integer quietusque iudex, plus est operis; sunt enim
omnia dicendo excitanda, nihil adjuvante natura. Sed tantum
vim habet illa, quae recte a bono poeta dicta est, flexanim atque
omnium regina rerum oratio, ut non modo inclinantem excipere
aut stantem inclinare, sed etiam adversantem ac repugnantem,
ut imperator fortis ac bonus, capere possit. [*De oratore* II. xliv.
187.]

("However, if the judge is unbiased, and free from passion,
the task is harder; for everything must then be called forth by
oratory, with no help from nature. But so great is the power of
eloquence, which was rightly called by a good poet, 'Incliner of
the soul, and queen of all things,' that it can not only make
straight one who is biased or bias one who is upright, but can
even, like a good and brave commander, make a prisoner of a
resisting opponent.")

It will be noted that the appeal is to *oratio*, not to *ratio*.

But the emotions of love, hate, fear, or pity appropriate to
the occasion must be somehow present in the speaker if he is
to excite those emotions in the hearers. The demands made
on him by his cases and subjects would seem to be so varied
that he would have to study and practice the art of the actor.
On the contrary, says Antonius, " . . . magna vis est earum
sententiarum atque eorum locorum quos agas tractesque dicendo, nihil ut opus sit simulatione et fallaciis. Ipsa enim
natura orationis eius, quae suscipitur ad aliorum animos per-
movendos, oratorem ipsum magis etiam, quam quemquam
eorum qui audiunt, permovet." ("So great is the force in those

thoughts and commonplaces which you handle and discuss in speaking that there is no need for pretense or deceit; for the very nature of the language which is adopted to move the passions of others moves the orator himself more than any one of his listeners.") (*De oratore* II. xlvi. 191.) His own speech intoxicates him!

Quintilian's views parallel those of Cicero. He recognizes the place of emotion in all parts of the speech; he emphasizes its importance in the exordium and in the peroration, two sections where *conciliare* and *movere* are especially to be sought.[12] He stresses once more the decisive part played by feelings in persuasion, and pares down correspondingly the importance of proofs: to affect the judge or listener, to cause him to weep, "Huc igitur incumbat orator, hoc opus ejus, hic labor est, sine quo cetera nuda, jejuna, infirma, ingrata sunt, adeo velut spiritus operis hujus atque animus est in affectibus." ("To this end, therefore, the orator must devote himself; this is his task and work; without this the rest is bare, spiritless, weak and unattractive; for the soul and the life, so to speak, of oratory are found in the emotions.") (*De institutione oratoria*, VI. ii. 7.) Finally, he asserts that one must feel the emotions to be communicated to one's audience. Here he goes beyond Cicero and proposes a technique for arousing oneself. By the power of imagination an orator or advocate can represent so vividly to himself the issues and acts of which he speaks that he becomes in effect a spectator and reacts as a spectator would.

The contrast is total with Port-Royal. On the one hand, the speaker whose mind and efforts are based on imposing his truth by argument, yes, but especially by force of character and by manipulation of feelings, and, on the other hand, the speaker who effaces himself, who wants no coloring of the *moi* to deflect the judgment of the listener, who leaves all or as much as possible to the force of reasons springing from the nature of things. The classical theory apparently invites

75

the audience to fall into and the speaker to bring about the very "sophismes d'amour propre, d'intérêt et de passion" against which the *Logique* supposedly gives protection.

The leading principle of the next discussion of sophisms is that one may take the appearance of the thing for the reality, the unimportant aspect of it for the essential part, the part which should motivate judgment. This brings us into a significant comparison of judgment in art and judgment in eloquence. "Aussi ceux qui sont intelligents dans la peinture estiment infiniment plus le dessein que le coloris ou la délicatesse du pinceau, néanmoins les plus ignorants sont plus touchés d'un tableau, dont les couleurs sont vives et éclatantes, que d'un autre plus sombre, qui serait admirable pour le dessein" (*Logique*, pp. 355–56). In passing, one should note the very strong preference implied in that "infiniment." The argument continues: in the judgment of paintings the ignorant are likely to defer to the expert, so the frequency of error is less notable than in other things where everyone feels free to judge, and such is the case with eloquence. "On appelle, par exemple, un prédicateur éloquent lorsque ses périodes dont bien justes, et qu'il ne dit point de mauvais mots; et sur ce fondement M. de Vaugelas dit en un endroit, qu'un mauvais mot fait plus de tort à un prédicateur ou un avocat qu'un mauvais raisonnement" (*Logique*, p. 556). The terms of the analogy begin to be clarified: drawing and color correspond to reasoning and words or expression.

But let us digress for a moment to note the reference to Vaugelas. His *Remarques sur la langue française* (of 1647, fifteen years before the first edition of the Port-Royal *Logique*) are obviously designed to fit into a rhetorical approach to language. He looks forward to the coming of a French Quintilian. In referring to Vaugelas, Arnauld and Nicole show us indirectly the actuality of their treatment of rhetoric; they were not simply attacking ancient authorities; they had their sights on contemporary and official representatives of the classical point of view.

One must believe, they go on to say, that Vaugelas was speaking of a matter of fact, of a situation that exists, but of which he does not approve. It is true that there are people who judge sermons and legal arguments in this way, " . . . mais il est vrai aussi qu'il n'y a rien de moins raisonnable que ces jugements: car la pureté du langage, le nombre des figures sont tout au plus dans l'éloquence, ce que le coloris est dans la peinture, c'est-à-dire, que ce n'en est que la partie la plus basse et la plus matérielle . . . " (*Logique*, p. 356).

What seemed to emerge in the discussion of figurative language—that the Port-Royalists would find little of interest in the part of rhetoric known as elocution—is confirmed here. Conceptions based on things, conceptions which speakers and writers transmit as they are, with all of their original liveliness—that is what Arnauld and Nicole want everyone to strive for, the one exception[13] being religious truths. There the *prédicateur* should try to express and to communicate the feelings with which he conceives those truths. Once more we find ourselves returning to the point that an artistic theory of expression is unnecessary and pernicious. Both clear conception and moving language may be found in people who have no special interest in words. In fact those two virtues are rare among those who apply themselves consciously to such matters.

. . . C'est ce qui se peut rencontrer en des personnes peu exactes dans la langue, et peu justes dans le nombre, et qui se rencontre même rarement dans ceux qui s'appliquent trop aux mots, et aux embellissements, parce que cette vue les détourne des choses, et affaiblit la vigueur de leurs pensées, comme les peintres remarquent que ceux qui excellent dans le coloris, n'excellent pas ordinairement dans le dessein, l'esprit n'étant pas capable de cette double application, et l'une nuisant à l'autre. [*Logique*, pp. 356–57.]

The ornamented language and especially the eloquence Cicero calls *abundantem sonantibus verbis uberibusque sententiis* may conceal falsities. The decorations not only make it harder for the audience to discern the truth; they actually lead speakers astray: be on your guard, say the Port–Royalists, when you hear an orator begin a long gradation or an antithesis with several members; his figures will probably cause him to twist the truth in order to make it fit the " . . . vain ouvrage de paroles qu'il veut former" (*Logique*, p. 358). "*Pointes,*" rhyme, Ciceronian expressions, allusions to pagan divinities (they ridicule Cardinal Bembo for saying that a pope had been elected by the favor of the immortal gods, *deorum immortalium beneficiis*)—all are sources of errors often unperceived by those who utter them, so dazzled are they by their own words.

It is here that the logicians make absolutely clear the aesthetic implications of their doctrine.

Les faux raisonnements de cette sorte que l'on rencontre si souvent dans les écrits de ceux qui affectent le plus d'être éloquents, font voir combien la plupart des personnes qui parlent, ou qui écrivent, auraient besoin d'être bien persuadées de cette excellente règle, qu'il n'y a rien de beau, que ce qui est vrai: ce qui retrancherait des discours une infinité de vains ornements et de pensées fausses. [*Logique*, p. 360.]

The argument for the "véritable rhétorique" reaches its climax at this point. It sets itself up in opposition to the theory of thought and expression that was at the same time being recovered and restated from the ancients. "Rien n'est beau que le vrai," the cardinal principle of French classicism, has one of its most vigorous expressions and justifications in this logic.

But the curious thing is that neither logic, as here conceived, nor rhetoric, as Aristotle, Cicero, and Quintilian conceived it, has a place for an independent beauty that is an end in itself. All concerned agree on that; they begin to differ when they say on what primary value beauty depends. With the Port–Royalists, it follows from truth; Quintilian represents the other side when he declares succinctly: "Numquam vera species ab utilitate dividitur." ("True beauty is never separate from utility.") (*De institutione oratoria* II. viii. 2.) With the former, truth is established by demonstration, with Quintilian by persuasion; and for both, beauty must be subordinate to the primary aim or technique. The overriding *utilitas* points to the heart of the matter for the rhetorician, who is basically skeptical. He is ready to make a case for either side of the question, and he is willing to consent to the verdict of a third party. For him truth comes out of a contest for someone's adherence to an opinion, and in that context what one decides to say is tested by the criterion of effectiveness in causing adherence. To the logician the nature of things and the nature of thought are decisive; truth emerges from the effort to bring the two into coincidence. Once achieved, the truth is laid before the third party, who is not expected to judge it, as though he stood above it, but rather to recognize it and to submit to it. The Port-Royalists are quite prepared to pay the price:

Il est vrai que cette exactitude rend le style plus sec et moins pompeux; mais elle le rend aussi plus vif, plus sérieux, plus clair, et plus digne d'un honnête homme: l'impression en est bien plus forte, et bien plus durable; au lieu que celle qui naît simplement de ces périodes si ajustées, est tellement superficielle, qu'elle s'évanouit presque aussitôt qu'on les a entendues. [*Logique*, p. 360.]

The "sophisme de l'autorité" and the "sophisme de la

manière" belong also in the category of mistaking some appearance or external mark for the reality or the truth. In the first of these, age or piety or moderation or wealth or rank or erudition or some other quality of the author is taken as a sign of truth and a stimulus of judgment. Since the minds of men are ordinarily "faibles et obscurs, pleins de nuages et de faux jours" (*Logique*, p. 365), they usually accept the views held by people having some visible qualification or title to authority. Although there is no necessary connection between the truth and such marks, this "voie de persuader" often prevails. Of course, Arnauld and Nicole make a distinction between legitimate authority and the unimportant or misleading kind. One must respect that of the Church in matters of faith and the mysteries of salvation, but elsewhere intrusions of authority are often causes of error.

> Mais dans les choses dont la connaissance n'est pas absolument nécessaire et que Dieu a laissées davantage au discernement de la raison de chacun en particulier l'autorité et la manière ne sont pas si considérables, et elles servent souvent à engager plusieurs personnes en des jugements contraires à la vérité. [*Logique*, p. 366.]

It will be readily noted that this treatment of authority is, from the point of view of rhetoric, another attack on the speaker as a means of persuasion. The suppression of the *moi* that, as we have seen, is required in argumentation for reasons of piety and *honnêteté* and the avoidance of authority in instances where such pressure is not called for: these two ideas complement and reinforce one another.

Actually the position of the Port-Royalists as regards the image and role of the speaker or writer has even a further nuance, one that allows them to assimilate as much as possible of the traditional concern for the sensibilities of the audience. Here I am thinking of their final chapter on the subject of bad reasoning in which they treat what they call "manière." By this term they mean something other than signs like age or piety as the bases of authority, and, also, something distinct from style. They are referring to a man's way of stating the truth, or, more specifically, to the moral attitude that underlies that way. For example, one is more inclined to believe the person who speaks easily, with gravity, moderation, and gentleness than to believe the person who shows anger, hostility, or presumption. Once more the authors of the *Logique* remind us that these external tokens may deceive; we in the audience must consider "manière" and "fond" separately.

Nevertheless, it is in connection with manner that Arnauld and Nicole enunciate what they call the greatest principle of rhetoric. One cannot but think that here they are drawing on bitter experience in the furore over Jansenius' book on Augustine and Pascal's *Lettres provinciales*. If it is reasonable to be on one's guard against deciding an issue on the basis of the way it is proposed, it is equally reasonable for the persuader to seek to clothe the truth in "manières favorables," that is, suitable for getting approval, and to avoid "manières odieuses" which would alienate men. Since no truth can be expounded without an accompanying manner, it cannot be neglected. I do not say that it should be *exploited*: for the Port-Royalists, one would then fall back into the habits of the Ciceronians. The aim must be to stay out of truth's way.

S'ils honorent sérieusement la vérité, ils ne doivent pas la déshonorer en la couvrant des marques de la fausseté et du mensonge: et s'ils l'aiment sincèrement ils ne doivent pas attirer sur elle la haine et l'aversion des hommes par la manière choquante dont ils la proposent. C'est le plus grand précepte de la rhétorique, qui est d'autant plus utile qu'il sert à régler l'âme aussi bien que les paroles. [*Logique*, p. 374.]

For Port-Royal, rhetoric is not the *method* of truth, as it tended to be in the tradition; it is only a means of easing the communication of truth once it has been found *by another method*. Aristotle's great achievement had been to formulate in his *Rhetoric* a dispassionate account of the means of persuasion that did not involve them in the requirements of scientific accuracy and in the commitment to any one truth. The Ciceronian tradition, though it insisted on an alliance of wisdom and eloquence in rhetoric, is ultimately skeptical or probabilistic on questions of truth. The Port-Royalists would have had a higher opinion of rhetoric if they had not held so high an opinion of truth, so firm a conviction of its attainability, and such confidence in its power to impose itself once grasped.

This *Logique* seriously intends, therefore, to improve and even replace rhetoric. The comments of its authors, made *en passant* as they develop their art of thought, have dealt so far with language (especially in its figurative uses), with commonplaces (as the principles with which invention begins), and with reasonings (insofar as they depend on things and on the manner and status of the speaker). Their manual appears at a time when seventeenth-century literary theory is beginning to crystallize into its clearest and, as we have come to say, its most obviously *classical* phase. The moment is well chosen for the kind of deliberate braking influence that this *Art de penser* seeks to exercise on the dominant Ciceronian trend. For the final implications of this attempt, we shall have to study the fourth and most original section of the work, the one entitled, "De la méthode."

1. *La Logique ou l'art de penser* (Paris, 1664), p. 28. All references, unless otherwise noted, are to this edition.

2. As a matter of fact, Arnauld and Nicole could have been (and, perhaps, were) inspired in their criticism and in their remedy by Quintlian, who is perfectly aware of such excesses. Cf., for example: " . . . Resistam iis, qui, omissa rerum (qui nervi sunt in causis) diligentia, quodam inani circa voces studio senescunt, idque faciunt gratia decoris, qui est in dicendo mea quidem opinione pulcherrimus, sed cum sequitur non cum affectatur." ("I must resist those who, failing to concern themselves with things and ideas, which are the sinews of pleadings, grow old in the futile study of words; they do so for the sake of elegance, which is, I agree, the most beautiful quality of style, but only when it is appropriate and not when it is affected.") (De institutione oratoria, VIII, proemium 18; the edition I am using is that of Henri Bornecque, in four volumes, Paris, n.d.) Or, again, at the end of the Proemium: "Sit igitur cura elocutionis quam maxima, dum sciamus tamen nihil verborum causa esse faciendum, cum verba ipsa rerum gratia sint reperta." ("Let us be as careful of form as possible, but let us recognize that one should do nothing merely for the sake of words, for the words themselves were invented for the sake of things to be expressed.") But we can be sure that the Port-Royalists did not share Quintilian's view of ornament (" . . . qui est in dicendo . . . pulcherrimus"); nor would they have emphasized admiration and pleasure as rhetorical aims. Quintilian does just that in the lines that follow immediately the second passage quoted.

3. Aeneid xii. 1. 646. But the authors of the Logique have before them, not Virgil, but Quintilian. In Book VIII, chap. v ("De generibus sententiarum"), we learn first that "Sententiam veteres, quod animo sensissent, vocaverunt." ("The ancients signified by the word sententia a feeling or opinion.") Later, in paragraphs 5 and 6 of the chapter, Quintilian offers two examples of plain declarations, one of which is: "Mors misera non est, aditus ad mortem est miser." He continues, "Sed majorem vim accipiunt et mutatione figurae, ut 'Usque adeone mori miserum est?' Acrius hoc enim quam per se: 'Mors misera non est!'" ("Death is not painful, but the approach to death." " . . . But the ideas take on greater force by a change in the figure: 'Is it, then, so painful to die?'—a form that is more vigorous than the simple statement: 'Death is not painful.'")

4. "Sed ne causae quidem parum confert idem hic orationis ornatus. Nam qui libenter audiunt et magis attendunt et facilius credunt, plerumque ipsa delectatione capiuntur, nonnumquam admiratione auferuntur." ("But the elegance of expression contributes also not a little to the success of the case. For those who listen with pleasure pay closer attention and believe us more easily; most of the time they are led along by this very pleasure; sometimes they are carried away by admiration.") (Bk. VIII, chap. iii, 5.)

5. Bk. II, chap. xli, 175. My references are to the edition of De oratore, ed. E Courbaud and H. Bornecque (Paris, 1956–59).

6. Cicero's position is opposed to this, of course, but it does not lack nuances. Crassus is made to say in De oratore I. xxxii. 146. "Verum ego hanc vim intellego esse in praeceptis omnibus, non ut ea secuti oratores eloquentiae laudem sint adepti, sed, quae sua sponte homines eloquentes facerent, ea quosdam observasse atque collegisse; sic esse non eloquentiam ex artificio, sed artificium ex eloquentia natum. Quod tamen, ut ante dixi, non eiicio; est enim, etiamsi minus necessarium ad bene dicendum, tamen ad cognoscendum non inliberale." ("But I consider the virtue and status of all rules to be this: not that orators by following them have won praise for eloquence, but that certain persons have noted and

collected what men of eloquence did of their own accord; so that eloquence has not sprung from art, but art from eloquence. However, as I said before, I do not reject art, for, though not necessary for oratory, it is still a liberal subject for study.") Antonius has similar things to say in Book II (e.g., in chap. viii. 32), and in both cases the reservations about the usefulness of the rules, especially in their more elaborate forms, make the factors of nature or original gift and practice more important in eloquence.

7. *Logique*, pp. 293–94. Here the authors of the *Logique* have very probably drawn their ammunition from Quintilian himself, as they had a few lines earlier, when they paraphrase and quote him as follows: "Aussi quoique Quintilien fasse paraître de l'estime pour cet art, il est obligé néanmoins de reconnaître qu'il ne faut pas, lorsqu'on traite une matière, aller frapper à la porte de tous les lieux pour en tirer des arguments et des preuves. Illud quoque studiosi eloquentiae cogitent, neque omnibus in causis ea, quae demonstravimus, cuncta posse reperiri, neque, cum proposita fuerit materia dicendi, scrutanda singula et velut ostiatim pulsanda, ut sciant, an ad probandum id, quod intendimus, forte respondeant; nisi cum discunt et adhuc usu carent" (p. 292). (" . . . Those who study eloquence should reflect on this fact, that they cannot find in all cases all of the forms of argument that we have indicated; and when a subject has been proposed for treatment, they should not examine all the headings successively and knock on every door, so to speak, to see whether they may give the proof that we seek—unless it be when they are learning and still lack practice.")

The passage in Quintilian continues: "Infinitam enim faciat ista res dicendi tarditatem, si semper necesse sit ut tentantes unum quodque eorum, quod sit aptum atque conveniens, experiendo noscamus; nescio an etiam impedimento futura sint, nisi et animi quaedam ingenita natura et studio exercitata velocitas recta nos ad ea, quae conveniunt causae, ferant." ("Such a situation would make the process of speaking infinitely slow, if it were always necessary for us to try out every one of the arguments and thus to learn by experiment what is suitable and appropriate; I am not sure that it would not be an obstacle to progress, unless a certain natural talent and a facility acquired by study lead us directly to the arguments that suit the case.") (*De institutione oratoria* V. x. 122–23.) From this it is clear that Quintilian's views are more balanced than one might suppose from the account in the *Logique*.

8. Especially notable in these lines: "J'estimais fort l'éloquence, et j'étais amoureux la poésie; mais je pensais que l'une et l'autre étaient des dons de l'esprit plutôt que des fruits de l'étude. Ceux qui ont le raisonnement le plus fort, et qui digèrent le mieux leurs pensées, afin de les rendre claires et intelligibles, peuvent toujours le mieux persuader ce qu'ils proposent, encore qu'ils ne parlassent que bas breton, et qu'ils n'eussent jamais appris de Rhétorique. Et ceux qui ont les inventions les plus agréables, et qui les savent exprimer avec le plus d'ornement et de douceur, ne laisseraient pas d'être les meilleurs poètes, encore que l'art poétique leur fût inconnu."—*Discours de la méthode*, ed. E. Gilson (Paris, 1947), p. 7.

9. Cited by Gilson, p. 185.

10. Descartes and Port-Royal agree on a related point—the criticism of the *Lullistes* (the followers of Raymond Lull, 1235–1315), who aspired, with the help of Lull's *Ars brevis*, to speak well on any and all subjects. Their starting points or "attributs généraux" were species of common-

places, according to the *Logique*. Descartes writes with scorn in the *Discours* of Lull's art; it helps one, he says, to speak without judgment of things one knows nothing about. Gilson gathers the evidence showing that Descartes considered Lull's method to be a scheme of reasoning based on commonplaces.

11. For this distinction, see, for example, *Rhetoric* I. ii. 1356ª 1–14. References are to *The Basic Works of Aristotle*, ed. Richard McKeon (New York, 1941).

12. See, e.g., in the *De institutione oratoria* IV, i, and VI, 1-11.

13. At least the only one noted in the context of logic.

Chapter IV

Port-Royal: Logic vs. Rhetoric (II)

𝔍L NOUS RESTE à expliquer la dernière partie de la logique, qui regarde la méthode, laquelle est sans doute l'une des plus utiles et des plus importantes" (*Logique*, p. 377). This introduces an impressive and novel section of the *Logique*. The three earlier parts are based on the traditional list of mental operations: conception, judgment, and reasoning. The last part adds, in effect, a fourth kind of mental activity, by means of which thoughts are arranged into a convincing sequence. We note the familiar de-emphasis on the syllogistic phase of thought and learn at last what will supersede it as the Port-Royalists define a new way of combining thoughts.

"Il sert de peu pour bien démontrer, de savoir les règles des syllogismes, qui est à quoi on manque très peu souvent; mais que le tout est de bien arranger ses pensées, en se servant de celles qui sont claires et évidentes, pour pénétrer dans ce qui paraissait plus caché" (*Logique*, p. 377). The work as a whole has a cumulative structure, each section depending for its materials on the one that precedes it. One consequence is that any treatment, such as would be found in most books of logic, that stops with the syllogism omits the most important step of all.

The general place of method in the treatise is unmistak-

ably clear: it is the last in a series of means to the end of truth
or, more exactly, to true knowledge (the French word is
science, as opposed to the vaguer term *connaissance*). In order
to grasp the exact place that Arnauld and Nicole assign to
method in their scheme, let us analyze this term *science*, for
the function of method is here (and everywhere, I assume)
intimately linked to the nature of the truth to be found. The
characteristic thing about this argument is its focus on assent,
and on the degrees and motivations of assent. (The essentially
simple and undifferentiated adhesion which might satisfy
the rhetorician is hardly sufficient here.) In considering a
statement or "maxime,"

1. one knows its truth because it is self-evident; we
are persuaded of it if it is without need of further reasoning; it is the kind of knowledge that the logicians call
intelligence (in English I should be inclined to call it
intuition); or

2. we feel the need for some other motive of assent;
and this category of "maxime" may be subdivided according to the nature of the supporting element that is
required:

a. if it is grounded on authority, the type of assent
is known as *foi*; or

b. if it is grounded on a reason or reasons, one will
find oneself

(1) in a state of imperfect conviction, which is
opinion; or

(2) in a state of perfect conviction, which may be

a. only apparent, in which case the name for
the state is *erreur*; or

b. real, and that is *science*.

Method is, therefore, the procedure which combines judgments in such a way as to produce knowledge in the sense just shown; and in so doing it must discover and then use self-evident principles—(*intelligence* in the special sense mentioned above); or again, and more simply, method is the path one follows in going from the clear and evident to the hidden and the unassented-to.

In practice it is useful to distinguish two methods, one for discovering the truth, the other for proving it to others when we have discovered it.

> Ainsi il y a deux sortes de méthodes; l'une pour découvrir la vérité, qu'on appelle *analyse* ou méthode de *résolution,* et qu'on peut aussi appeler méthode d'*invention;* et l'autre pour la faire entendre aux autres quand on l'a trouvée, qu'on appelle *synthèse* ou méthode de *composition,* et qu'on peut aussi appeler méthode de *doctrine.*
>
> On ne traite pas d'ordinaire par analyse le corps entier d'une science, mais on s'en sert seulement pour résoudre quelque question. [*Logique,* p. 391.]

For the Port-Royalists, there is obviously no necessity for a doctrine or method of *expression.* In addressing someone with the aim of winning his assent, one uses essentially the same method as one used in establishing the truth in the first place. The synthetic and analytic procedures are, in fact, merely different movements along the same line; and in either case, the power of proof comes from linearity of thought, from strict observance of the order in which principles and consequences occur. In analysis, one searches for the antecedent or antecedents upon which a given affirmation depends for its cogency. In synthesis one reverses the direction: both antecedents and consequents being known, one simply displays their interrelationship to the person to be taught. There is no rhetorical adjustment of the truth to him; he grasps the truth in the same way as the scientist or specialist does.

We may, therefore, take as the basis of the rest of our

discussion the synthetic method, which is " . . . la plus importante en ce que c'est celle dont on se sert pour expliquer toutes les sciences" (*Logique,* p. 402). Descartes' four rules are quoted in connection with analysis, but the authors of the *Logique* believe that they are " . . . générales pour toutes sortes de méthodes et non particulières pour la seule analyse" (*Logique,* p. 401). Like Descartes, however, they find in geometry the model for method.

> Il y a encore beaucoup de choses à observer pour rendre cette méthode parfaite et entièrement propre à la fin qu'elle se doit proposer, qui est de nous donner une connaissance claire et distincte de la vérité. Mais parce que les préceptes généraux sont plus difficiles à comprendre quand ils sont séparés de toute matière, nous considérerons la méthode que suivent les géomètres, comme étant celle qu'on a toujours jugée la plus propre pour persuader la vérité, et en convaincre entièrement l'esprit. [*Logique,* pp. 402–3.]

It is easy to state the three characteristics or conditions that must be fulfilled in the method: (1) there must be no ambiguity in terms; (2) reasoning must begin from clear and evident principles; and (3) one must demonstrate every conclusion that is advanced. At once the controversial relationship with rhetoric emerges.[1]

> Ne laisser aucun des termes un peu obscur ou équivoque sans le définir. . . .
> N'employer dans les définitions que des termes parfaitement connus ou déjà expliqués. . . .
> N'abuser jamais de l'équivoque des termes en manquant d'y substituer mentalement les définitions qui les restreignent et qui les expliquent. [*Logique,* p. 404.]

Again and again Arnauld and Nicole insist on clarity, explicitness, and univocity of terms, the last of these being truly the *sine qua non* of their method. But one has only to read casually in Book I of Aristotle's *Rhetoric*, e.g., in chaps. 5, 6, 7, 9, 10, where the notions of happiness, good, utility, vice, virtue, and wrongdoing are introduced in the way proper to the orator, in order to see the unavoidable ambiguity of the terms which will serve as basic predicates in rhetorical reasoning. Notice his remarks on happiness: "We may define happiness as prosperity combined with virtue; or as independence of life; or as the secure enjoyment of the maximum of pleasure; or as a good condition of property and body, together with the power of guarding one's property and body and making use of them. That happiness is one or more of these things, pretty well everyone agrees."[2] Whoever tries to eliminate this ambiguity simply confuses rhetoric with science, according to Aristotle's view. To make such an attempt means that one has failed to see that the starting points of arguments must be either special and peculiar to one category of things— like the principles of a particular science—or that, in certain situations (as in rhetoric), they must be common, that is, so conceived that they can be made to fit many or all sorts of things.[3]

Cicero understands very well the need for flexible, multivalent starting points. More than once in *De oratore* he has Antonius emphasize the tendency of the well-trained and experienced orator to return, no matter how varied the circumstances, to a small number of headings as he puts his case together and argues it. There is a curious passage in the dialogue where we learn of three aspects which may be isolated in a matter under debate, aspects recognizable in the answers given to these three questions: was the deed done?, what was done?, and of what sort or quality was it? The second of these requires an act of definition. As an example, Antonius refers to a case in which everything turned on the sense of the word *maiestas*. Neither advocate sought to define precisely the term at issue, as they might have done if they had followed the advice of some teachers.

Quod mihi quidem perquam puerile videri solet. Alia est enim, cum inter doctos homines de eis ipsis rebus quae versantur in artibus disputatur, verborum definitio, ut quom quaeritur quid sit ars, quid sit lex, quid sit civitas. In quibus hoc praecipit ratio et doctrina, ut vis eius rei quam definias sic exprimatur ut neque absit quicquam neque supersit. [*De oratore* II. xxv. 108.]

("This advice seems to me very puerile, for the definition of words is quite a different thing when a dispute arises among specialists about matters treated in the sciences, as when one inquires, what is an art, what is a law, what is a state? In these circumstances reason and method direct that the nature of the thing which you define should be expressed in such a manner that there will be nothing lacking or superfluous.")

Instead, both speakers used all the resources of rhetorical amplification on the content of the phrase *maiestatem minuere*. Risking a formal definition might have given to the opponent the chance to add something damaging, or to subtract or modify something; and the initiative would thus pass to other hands. In any case, there is a scholastic air about such an exercise, something almost childish. Finally, and worst of all, it is ineffective; it does not really make an impression on the mind of the judge; it escapes him before he grasps it. And so the contrast goes: on the one side, that of logic, insistence on exactness and singleness of meaning; on the other, a desire to use in argument the possibilities of analogy, of flexibility in application, even of imprecision.

As for principles, the Port-Royalists want to begin with axioms, with individual acts of judgment in which subject and predicate are seen to be joined inescapably. They offer at one point a list of eleven such principles. "Clear and indubitable" (*Logique*, p. 424), these truths may serve as the basis ("fondement") for knowing the most hidden things. Here are three of them: "Tout ce qui est enfermé dans l'idée claire et distincte d'une chose, en peut être affirmé avec vérité." " . . . Le néant ne peut être cause d'aucune chose." " . . . Il est de la nature d'un esprit fini de ne pouvoir comprendre l'infini." (*Logique,* pp. 425, 427.) But the rhetorician or orator—as, for example, in the theory of Aristotle—looks neither at things nor within himself in order to discover his principles. He looks rather to his audience and to the opinions it holds, to its fund of common knowledge. Most of the first book of the *Rhetoric* consists, in fact, of summaries of such knowledge, as I have indicated above. In Book II, the treat- ment of maxims as the premises or conclusions of enthymemes reveals the same tendency in Aristotle's advice—to look for the commonly accepted opinions: "The maxim, as has been already said, is a general statement, and people love to hear stated in general terms what they already believe in some particular connexion. . . . The orator has therefore to guess the subjects on which his hearers hold views already, and what these views are, and then must express, as general truths, these same views on these same subjects." [4]

From univocal definitions and self-evident premises, the discussion in the *Logique* moves to demonstration itself. As the act of combining the known with the unknown in such a way that the latter follows from the former, its characteristic qualities are order and completeness. In a first set of rules for demonstrations, we read: "Prouver toutes les propositions un peu obscures en n'employant à leur preuve que les défini- tions qui auront précédé, ou les axiomes qui auront été accordés, ou les propositions qui auront déjà été démontrées, ou la construction de la chose même dont il s'agira, lorsqu'il y aura quelque opération à faire" (*Logique,* p. 404). This advice or precept, which regards mainly the *rigor* of the demonstration, is later supplemented in another enumeration by two other "règles pour la méthode," which stress further the need for sequence and add the requirement of *exhaustiveness*.

> Traiter les choses autant qu'il se peut dans leur ordre naturel, en commençant par les plus générales et les plus simples, et expliquant tout ce qui appartient à la nature du genre, avant de passer aux espèces particulières.
> Diviser autant qu'il se peut chaque genre en toutes ses espèces, chaque tout en toutes ses parties, et chaque difficulté en tous ses cas. [*Logique,* p. 443.]

The ideal is to define everything and to prove everything (unless what one starts with is certain in itself). Arnauld and Nicole know quite well that they are describing an ideal performance, one that can be only approximated in fact: the repeated phrase *autant qu'il se peut* has an operative value, not merely a decorative one. But because one must always reckon with the limits of the human mind and with the often elusive characteristics of things does not weaken the ideal for them. Its attractive power remains intact.

It is not difficult to find the points of contact between this theory of demonstration and rhetorical theory. They come together at the point where rhetorical arrangement, the operation following on invention, is investigated. Nor is it hard to understand the antagonism between these two approaches to the subject of combining arguments into convincing or persuasive units. Rigor and natural order in the one is set off against a looser organization in the other, against a tentative plan that may vary decidedly with the circumstances and according to the judgment of the orator. It is the notion of a chain of propositions versus the notion of a sum or total. A speech has, of course, a "natural" order, from *exordium* to *narratio* to *confirmatio* to *refutatio* to *peroratio;* it moves from introduction to statement of the act and issues to presentation of proofs and refutations to conclusion. But this order, though logical and usual, may be changed by rearranging the parts or even by suppressing one or more of them.[5] From my reading of Quintilian I conclude that the only fixed position in the scheme is that of the peroration. This takes us quite far from the insistence on gradual progression from genus to species or from whole to part that Arnauld and Nicole felt to be necessary. Morever, both exordium and peroration are extraneous from the point of view of logic, since they lie outside of the effort to demonstrate; from the point of view of rhetoric, they are entirely pertinent as the places in which the speaker exerts himself to gain the attention, good will, and docility (in the strict sense of the word) of the judge and, at the end, to restate his case quickly and impressively.[6]

In the narration one should aim at clarity, brevity, and probability (and incidentally, this third term indicates that one will settle for something less than deductive certainty); one should avoid, Quintilian continues, contradictions and inconsistencies; but he adds that if anyone needs this bit of advice he might as well give up the study of the rhetorician's art. In other words, he takes as obvious the central topic of the Port-Royalists and goes on from there. As a very real possibility, one may consider inserting a digression at the end of the narration—something not completely detached, of course, but a brilliant amplification of some theme that has been touched upon, or something like a second exordium to make sure that one has the ear and sympathy of the audience (De institutione oratoria IV. iii). Digressions may be placed to advantage in other parts of the text or speech.

Under the heading of proofs, one notes that signs and symbols prove as surely as arguments and groups of arguments do; and to these we must add the whole category of "atechnical" means of persuasion, such as documents, wit-

95

nesses, and the like. Again, Quintilian realizes as well as anyone that argumentation requires principles, things taken for granted at the outset. Here he lists the ones that are certain:

> Pro certis autem habemus primum quae sensibus percipiuntur, ut quae videmus, audimus, qualia sunt signa; deinde ea, ad quae communi opinione consensum est, deos esse, praestandam pietatem parentibus; praeterea, quae legibus cauta sunt, quae persuasione etiam si non omnium hominum, ejus tamen civitatis aut gentis, in qua res agitur, in mores recepta sunt, ut pleraque in jure non legibus, sed moribus constant; si quid inter utramque partem convenit, si quid probatum est, denique cuicumque adversarius non contradicit. [*De institutione oratoria* V. x. 12–13.]

> ("But we take as certain, in the first place, things perceived by the senses, for instance, things that we see or hear, such as signs; secondly, those things on which there is general agreement, such as the existence of the gods and the duty of honoring one's parents; thirdly, things that are established by laws or that have been received as customary, if not by all men at least by the nation or state where the case is being pleaded—for many rights depend not on law but on custom; and finally, those things that both parties accept or that have been proved or that the adversary does not contradict.")

He concerns himself much less with what is self-evident than with what is indisputable or, rather, *undisputed in fact*. If an argument is accepted without further proof, that suffices; it may then play the role of an initial principle in the act of demonstrating.

The division of proofs into strong and weak, to which Quintilian refers (in Bk. V, chap. xii), is singularly out of harmony with the logical spirit, as is the discussion that follows from the distinction. One may, for example, give an appearance of strength to weak arguments by grouping them in a single development. Or, again, suppose that the speaker faces choices such as these: should the strongest arguments be put at the end of the proof?, or part of the strong ones at the end, as Homer does, with the weak in between?[7] Quintilian limits himself to this *dictum:* follow the order required by the particular case, but avoid a descending progression from strong to weak arguments.

On all of the foregoing points—the loose definition of proof, the pragmatic nature of its principles, the division and ordering of arguments—the attitude and theory of the rhetorician run counter to those of the logicians of Port-Royal.

In Chapter III and in the preceding pages, I have reviewed and analyzed the particular comments made by the authors of the *Logique* on the subject of rhetoric. By means of parallel citations and developments from the best known ancient treatises, I have defined, in passing, the issue and some of its implications. In the case of method—understood in the narrow sense given the term by the Port-Royalists, even though they do not work out explicitly the consequences of this notion for rhetoric—I have attempted to do so because they seem to me inevitable. I should like to draw together into a final and systematic statement my view of this conflict between logic and rhetoric and then to sketch the broad context into which the controversy fits. In 1662, we are obviously at a critical point in the history and application of two disciplines or intellectual styles. We have the good fortune to have on both sides the basic documents containing the fully elaborated positions. They are not contemporary, it is true; there had not yet appeared with unmistakable authority the expected French Quintilian. But the Latin one was very much alive, both in the *collèges* and outside of them; Patru was active; Bary had published, in 1659, his *Rhétorique française;* in 1664 (the date, incidentally, of the second edition of the *Logique,* with its strongly polemic "Second discours"), Rapin was to launch his series of comparisons and reflections with a volume on

97

Homer and Virgil. We see thus the emergence into intellectual consciousness of a contrast between methods that exclude each other when stated in their pure forms; though at the hands of lesser thinkers and critics, they undergo varying degrees of compromise and confusion.

A word about terminology is necessary at this point. Until now in this chapter, I have used "method" as referring to a part of logic, the crowning part in the constitution of a science, since it regulates the task of joining terms and affirmations into demonstrations, and I have made it analogous to arrangement in my comparison of the Port-Royalists with Aristotle, Cicero, and Quintilian. But in what follows, I should like to use the word in a broader sense, so that the logic of Port-Royal, with its four operations, is one method, and rhetoric, with its five stages (to adopt the analysis of Cicero and Quintilian), is another and, in this instance, an opposed method.

1. Let us assume, then, that both methods are designed to cause someone to assent to a truth. Logic focusses on one part of the person addressed, the intellectual part. So does rhetoric—is it not concerned with teaching and proving?— but it aims at a more comprehensive agreement, one involving imagination, feeling, will.

2. The truth that is accepted in each case differs: that which one reaches by logic is in fact known from the outset, at least virtually, in the definitions and premises; that which results from the processes of rhetoric is not known until the debate is over and a verdict rendered. And if one looks at the truths, not genetically, but in themselves, that of logic is, in the typical and decisive case, a judgment that cannot be doubted; that of rhetoric is an opinion molded by and adapted to particular circumstances; it has, therefore, no lasting hold on the mind of the judge (or listener or reader).

3. In both cases we are concerned with sequences: in logic, with sequences of thoughts based on principles that are simple, unambiguous, and objective; in rhetoric, with sequences of actions both mental and verbal based on starting points that may be clear or ambiguous, objective or not, provided they are effective.

4. The initial drives of the two methods—toward simplicity, on the one hand, and toward effectiveness, on the other—are applied to characteristically different materials: in logic, to *ideas* which have not only unvarying identities as terms in reasoning but also unvarying references to aspects of things ("Tout ce qui est enfermé dans l'idée claire et distincte d'une chose en peut être affirmé"); in rhetoric, to the *audience* and its baggage of notions, maxims, dispositions, and feelings, which may or may not be in conformity with things. In such a situation, the logician tends to see careless verbalizing in the works of his opponent; while the orator criticizes the logician for irrelevant and unattractive technicality.

5. The techniques by which the aspirations of the two methods are satisfied in the solution of problems differ markedly, although each one treats at least partially everything that the other treats. Each method analyzes inquiry or activity in its own way: in logic, the phases are conception, judgment, reasoning, method; in rhetoric, they are invention, arrangement, elocution, memory, and delivery. These enumerations, however blank they may seem, suggest an essential point. Logic is a series of mental acts in the course of which truth is discovered and established, with provision being made for communicating the truth to other minds once it is known and after error-causing influences such as prejudice or self-interest have been eliminated. Rhetoric is a set of procedures guiding a personal transaction between speakers and hearers in the course of which a position is advanced, justified, and

made appealing, with provision being made for the use of demonstrative proof as one of several kinds of persuasive devices.

6. The end results of applying the two methods are exactly opposed. As here understood, logic leads (if it is carried far enough) to the formation of a unified science that replaces other attempts to state what is known, attempts usually marked by vagueness and irregularity. On the other hand, rhetoric, because of the freedom it allows in invention and expression and because of its respect for what is particular in cases and circumstances, tends to produce many differing opinions, all credible to some degree; its justifications and decisions are never exclusive in any final sense.

7. Consequently, each method has its special attitude toward dialogue and controversy. The logician aims to eliminate controversy, since it is a sign of inadequate knowledge; and he distrusts unresolved dialogue, since the truth is one—or, at least, he hopes to make it so. The rhetorician thrives on controversy; and in moments of leisure—one thinks at once of Cicero—he takes pleasure in dialogue.

Through these documents one catches sight of an inevitable and far-reaching rivalry between two conceptions of the truth and between two ways of finding and supporting the truth. Because of the universality of the notions involved, the possible repercussions—in morality, in science, in history, in literature—are infinite. In fact, both rhetoric and logic, as we see them here and in antiquity, tend deliberately to expand their claims. Each starts with a relatively limited area or province, and then a kind of imperialism begins. In the *Gorgias* and *Phaedrus* of Plato, for example, rhetoric is hemmed in by the standards of justice and dialectic. Aristotle's view does not require the eventual transformation of rhetoric into dialectic upon which Plato insists; he finds a place for it as a method of dealing with problems, usually practical ones, where scientific solutions are not possible and where more than one opinion may be justified. It is not to be confused with logic or poetics or politics, though it has some of the characteristics of those disciplines and even borrows from them. However, in the theories of the professional Greek rhetoricians and, later, in those of Cicero and Quintilian, rhetoric asserts its claims to universality as a method. And not without plausibility: the Socratic or Platonic objection is answered, Cicero thinks, by the fact that, when truly understood, rhetoric does not simply train speakers in the technique of expression; it presupposes a joining of eloquence to wisdom. Thanks to wisdom, rhetoric can claim universal relevance; thanks to eloquence, it has a special dignity as the science that makes wisdom effective, that actually introduces true or probable insights into the fabric of human affairs.

The expansionism of logic is no less marked. It pervades the Cartesianism that inspires the fourth part (in particular) of the *Logique:* the model of knowledge and hence of method may be seen in geometry, the one place where there are agreed-upon truths and conclusive demonstrations. What the Port-Royalists wish to do is to extend, by suitable generalization, the way of geometry to all scientific inquiries and, beyond that, to judgment and reasoning as factors in everyday life. We cannot doubt that Arnauld and Nicole recognized this conflict of attitudes, aims, and procedures between rhetoric and logic—not perhaps in terms so purely opposed as the ones I have used above, but the fact is that, as they felt and conceived the issue, it could be resolved only by the substitution of logic for rhetoric and not by tolerance or compromise.

There is a curious resemblance and difference to be noted here. It has to do with the discipline of grammar. According to Quintilian, the art of rhetoric builds on a foundation laid down by the art of grammar. In the course of his early training, the future orator must learn his language and how to express himself correctly in it. Exercises in literary analysis and appreciation are important parts of this conception of grammar. The work of the professor of rhetoric assumes that of the professor of grammar, the two disciplines being conceived so as to fit together in a sequential order. Now, in 1660, Lancelot and Arnauld published their *Grammaire générale et raisonnée*. This was two years before the appearance of the *Logique,* but the doctrine of the later work harmonizes perfectly with that of the earlier one. In the grammar, for example, the parts of speech are analyzed and defined by reference to mental acts which are, as we find out later in the logic, none other than conception and judgment. In other words, the grammar of Port-Royal leads to *logic* and not to *rhetoric* as in the ancient plan. Arnauld and Nicole see no necessity for adding an art of expression, the effect of which is simply to encourage false and hyperbolic thoughts and forced figures. "Or l'on trouvera peut-être autant de choses utiles dans cette logique pour connaître et pour éviter ces défauts que dans les livres qui en traitent expressément" (*Logique,* p. 28).

It would be wrong, incidentally, to give the impression that rhetoric is the only art or discipline criticized in the important "Second discours" (or, for that matter, in the body of the treatise itself). There are substantial paragraphs on ethics, metaphysics, and physics. The authors claim that they have elucidated the general principles of each of these sciences in such a way as to eliminate errors and prejudices and to prepare the way for accurate judgment in these fields. They make a very ambitious statement to the effect that although their readers will not find in the *Logique* all that it is necessary for them to *know* in relation to these subjects, they will find there almost all that they need to *remember*. Even so, the position of rhetoric is especially precarious. After all, the Port-Royalists do acknowledge that we cannot give up entirely the books that treat technically the subject matters of morals, physics, and metaphysics. As for rhetoric, the only art really required is a discipline that restrains natural tendencies of thought and expression; and logic suffices for that.

The aim of replacing rhetoric becomes particularly plausible when the Port-Royalists propose logic as a way of teaching. It is not exclusively a tool for scientists. "La logique est l'art de bien conduire sa raison dans la connaissance des choses, tant pour s'en instruire soi-même, que pour en instruire les autres" (*Logique*, p. 39). In rhetoric, one starts characteristically with what we now think of as an "inter-personal" situation and with the things which must be done by the speaker or thinker as he addresses another party. In the logic of the Port-Royalists, one starts with the individual thinker and his effort to know things, but one eventually rejoins one's fellow man—*without a change of method*—since logic can solve the problems of communication and persuasion, too.

Something even more insidious, in a sense, is that the Port-Royalists have taken care not to make their new discipline repellent because of subtlety and complexity. They explain in the last pages of the "Premier discours" why they have omitted a number of items from the usual list of topics in logical treatises. The really useful things are included, such as the division of terms and ideas, certain reflections on propositions, and the rules for the use of figurative language. Some more abstruse and less useful topics, such as the conversion of propositions and the demonstration of syllogistic figures, are nevertheless discussed; they may be skipped by the reader, but, if covered, they exercise the mind, making it habitually more attentive. On the other hand, a great number of traditional questions having to do with subjects like the "universal *a parte rei*," "beings of reason," "second intentions" have disappeared without a trace. The authors had as their original intention to compose something simple enough and short enough to be read and learned quickly.

> La naissance de ce petit ouvrage est due entièrement au hasard, et plutôt à une espèce de divertissement qu'à un dessein sérieux. Une personne de condition entretenant un jeune seigneur, qui dans un âge peu avancé faisait paraître beaucoup de solidité et de pénétration d'esprit, lui dit qu'étant jeune il avait trouvé un homme qui l'avait rendu en quinze jours capable de répondre d'une partie de la logique. Ce discours donna occasion à une autre personne qui était présente, et qui n'avait pas grande estime de cette science, de répondre en riant que si Monsieur . . . en voulait prendre la peine, on s'engagerait bien de lui apprendre en quatre ou cinq jours tout ce qu'il y avait d'utile dans la logique.[8]

The plan decided upon was to make for the young gentleman (the Duc de Chevreuse) an abstract from the common logics that would be more concise and more exact than the original works. The job turned out to be more demanding than it had seemed at first. New reflections presented themselves, and instead of an abstract a new logic was the result. Nevertheless, the undertaking succeeded, for the young man, without a tutor and by using four tables, each of which was the business of one day, learned what he needed to know. And at the end of the first discourse, the authors assert that all others who are "somewhat advanced" will be able to read and learn this logic in seven or eight days!

The accident that explains the genesis of this remarkable book points to the secret of its enormous success. The Port-Royalists are, as usual, playing to win in the competition for the interest of all intelligent readers, speakers, and writers of the century. According to them, their logic will do what rhetoric failed to do as regards thinking and do with stricter conscience what rhetoric was supposed to do as regards communication. Moreover, and this is one of the greatest achievements of Arnauld and Nicole, their "art de penser" can be read by and speaks directly to an unspecialized audience that has become very sensitive to pedantry. In this virtue of accessibility, there lies, perhaps, a certain revenge. This improvement, this victory that the authors imagined—could it be pure? Were they not offering to the public a *rhetorical version* of logic? Is logic logic when it has been designed and composed so as to be learned easily by a "jeune seigneur" who is pressed for time? If, as Zeno is alleged to have said, logic is the clenched fist and rhetoric the extended hand, which is this?

I should like to suggest in conclusion a way of looking at the whole picture of critical thinking and theorizing in the decades from 1635 to 1685, with which I have been mainly concerned in the preceding chapters. On the first level of an imaginary scale, one may put the great majority of audiences and readers: these are people who have little or no theoretical interest in the rules and disciplines that underlie poetry, eloquence, and other forms of expression, and for whom criticism is informal judgment according to taste. At one remove from these, we may locate the occasional and basically unsystematic critics. Their production is large; they write observations, reflections, discourses, and dialogues.[9] Through the resulting assortment of judgments, maxims, and often ill-digested learning, one catches repeated glimpses of an aspiration toward lucidity in the treatment of literature according to rhetorical criteria. But this lucidity is achieved only on a third level, the level where we meet the authors of treatises: Bary, Le Gras, Rapin (to mention the most im-

portant figures), and, of course, their Greek and Latin authorities. It is here that problems of invention and style
emerge into the open and that one finds a serious effort to
state within the framework of a discipline the implications
of the principles (such as *nature* and *art*) brought to bear
on them.

But on this third level and in the midst of this discussion,
unquestionably dominated by rhetoric, there suddenly erupts
a competing discipline, logic. Its origins are certainly Cartesian; but it owes its effectiveness to the masterful *vulgarisa-
tion* of the Port-Royalists. In their treatise and in those of
the rhetoricians, as in clear mirrors, we can see reflected one
of the deepest tensions of French thought in the seventeenth
century, and, more specifically, one of the decisive periods
in the evolution of French literature—the early 1660's. These
works allow us to grasp in intellectual terms (and subject,
alas, to the limitations of such terms) something essential in
French classicism. I mean that, seen abstractly, it proceeds
from a balance of rhetorical and logical attitudes. In it the
possibilities of emptiness and servility that go with a search
for elegance, accessibility, and *bienséance* are balanced by
efforts to reach and state a truth that is more than relative and
to guard that truth against any drive on the part of expression
to become an end in itself.

To complete the picture, I should be inclined to add a
fourth level, on which all reference to authors ancient or
modern would be dropped in favor of anonymous (though
not unspecified) points of view. The achievements of the
great authorities could then be understood as deriving, by
ways known to intellectual creativity, from insights and ideals
that belong, in part, of course, to Aristotle and Cicero and
Port-Royal but have also an independent reality that stands
outside of time. Individual thinkers in concrete historical situations (to borrow an expression from Sartre) commit them-

selves to these attitudes with more or less *clairvoyance* and elaborate them as best they can, without ever realizing completely and definitively the possibilities of logic or of rhetoric, as the case may be. One sign of the extratemporality of these ideals lies precisely in that they recur from time to time as sources of theory and creation. I have just referred to Sartre; his example and that of Camus are instructive. There is plenty of justification, I think, for saying that in an essay like "Qu'est-ce que la littérature?", Sartre defines, in effect, literature as rhetorical activity that starts from the commonplaces of Marxism, and also that Camus, to judge from his *Discours de Suède,* adopts the notion of a literary art that ideally affects innumerable readers, bringing them together not, of course, with the Sartrian aims of removing feelings of innocence and irresponsibility in the class struggle but with the aim of helping them to sense the dignity and pathos of human brotherhood.

When, therefore, the seventeenth-century theorists of prose began to see their problems with sufficient clarity and to raise formally questions concerning truth and expression, they were working a vein that had produced before (they had, in fact, chosen it for that reason). It was productive again for them, although they had not foreseen the contest with logic. As later centuries were to discover, the vein had still further uses and was subject to other surprises.[10]

1. In their treatment of method the Port-Royalists do not themselves take up the discipline of rhetoric apropos of these conditions. But I have thought it useful to develop the contradictions here also. The disagreements already seen (in Chapter III) concerning the characters and motives of speakers, the commonplaces, the use of figurative style, and the exciting of passions are thus completed with regard to two important phases of rhetoric, invention and arrangement. By this extrapolation I hope to underline further the radical nature of the conflict between logic and rhetoric.

2. *The Basic Works of Aristotle,* ed. Richard McKeon (New York, 1941), 1360^b 15–20. 1339.

3. See *ibid.*, 1358^a 21–22. 1334.

4. *Ibid.*, II. 21. 1395^b 5–12. 1416.

5. See *De institutione oratoria* IV. ii. 4, 24.

6. *Ibid.*, IV. i. 5; *ibid.*, VI. i. 1–2, 7 *et seq.*

7. *Ibid.*, V. xii. 4–5, 14.

8. Page 1 of the "Avis."

9. On the subject of eloquence I have in mind authors and works like: Le P. Charles de Saint-Paul, *Tableau de l'éloquence française* (1657); R. Bary, *Actions publiques sur la rhétorique française* (1658); N. de Hauteville, *L'Art de bien discourir* (1666); G. Guéret, *Entretiens sur l'éloquence de la chaire et du barreau* (1666); Le Sieur de Richesource, *La Rhétorique du Barreau* (1668) and his *L'Eloquence de la chaire* (1673); D'Aubignac, *Discours académique sur l'éloquence* (1668); J. Carel de Sainte-Garde, *Réflexions académiques sur les poètes* (1676); and two anonymous pieces in *Divers traitez d'histoire, de morale et d'éloquence* (1672) entitled "L'Orateur" (apparently by Guéret) and "Si l'empire de l'Eloquence est plus grand que celui de l'Amour." Here is the cautious conclusion of the last-mentioned item: "Concluons donc, que l'Eloquence est toute puissante, et que l'Amour est toujours victorieux avec elle; ne divisons point leur autorité, et reconnaissons qu'ils se prêtent mutuellement leur assistance: si l'on dit que l'Amour rend éloquent, ajoutons que l'Eloquence rend amoureux, de leurs empires n'en faisons qu'un seul, et si nous admirons l'Eloquence, craignons l'Amour" (p. 129).

10. In saying "centuries," I am thinking of the eighteenth as well as the twentieth. I hope to analyze in another series of studies the ways in which the *philosophes* reinterpreted rhetoric and applied it to their problems of communication.

Chapter V

Pascal's Two Arts of Persuasion

For MOST READERS the two principal achievements of Pascal are the *Lettres provinciales* and the fragments we call the *Pensées*. Neither of these works can be considered as purely literary in the sense of having within itself its end and justification. Pascal created them as means of persuasion and their essential characteristics derive from this overriding aim. In trying to interpret them, we find ourselves pushed back inevitably to questions of rhetorical technique; we are obliged to make explicit conceptions of method that we have either brought to the works or discovered in Pascal. If we take the latter choice, we look for signs of method in the texts and, in the *Pensées* at least, we soon note many useful indications. The *Lettres provinciales* offer fewer guidelines; in regard to this work especially, we turn with interest to other writings of Pascal and, in particular, to the two important fragments on method usually published under the general title *De l'esprit géométrique*, the second one usually being referred to as "L'Art de persuader," the subtitle that Desmolets gave it in 1728.[1]

If we are to see the relationship between these two fragments and the *Provinciales* (without forgetting, of course, the *Pensées*), we must face at once three questions: (1) What is the relationship between the documents? (2) On what principles are they based? (3) What are their practical implications? I intend to deal here with all of these, but mainly with the second and third, since the answer to the first, though hard to give circumstantially in terms of dates and external events, becomes fairly easy when one passes to the second problem, that of analyzing the texts.

According to Brunschvicg, the probable story runs as follows: we know from Nicole's preface to Arnauld's *Nouveaux éléments de géométrie* (published in 1667, but the preparation of it goes back to 1660) that Pascal had composed an "Essai d'éléments de géométrie," which he later abandoned apparently because Arnauld objected to the order of the demonstrations. The two fragments we are concerned with here seem to have been written as a preface to this discarded work or, better, were drafts ("deux ébauches successives") of what was to be its preface. Brunschvicg dates it—the date is "tout à fait approximative," he says—as belonging to the winter of 1658–59. Chevalier follows this account, but tends to move the date further back. In his chronological table at the entry for 1657, he says that "vers cette époque" *De l'esprit géométrique* was composed as a preface to a treatise; and, emphasizing the theme of the *double infini*, which figures importantly in the first fragment, he relates the contents of the piece to problems with which Pascal was preoccupied as early as 1654. There is then a somewhat shaky case for believing that Pascal composed the two pieces for a single occasion—that is, as the preface for a geometry textbook.

However, since the discussion is not continuous, since the "first" fragment—on the *esprit géométrique* or the spirit of geometry—does not lead directly into the "second"—on the art of persuading—there is further need to justify the usual practice of printing the two texts side by side, or the more radical solution of Chevalier, who prints them as a single text divisible, after a short introductory paragraph, into a Section I and a Section II. A very useful hint comes from the Port-Royal *Logique*. In the "Discours sur le dessein de cette logique," which appears at the beginning of the first edition (1662), one reads:

> On a aussi tiré quelques autres réflexions d'un petit écrit non imprimé, qui avait été fait par un excellent esprit et qu'il avait intitulé, de l'*Esprit Géométrique*, et c'est ce qui est dit dans le chapitre X de la première partie, de la différence des définitions de nom et des définitions de chose, et les cinq règles, qui sont expliquées dans la quatrième partie, que l'on y a beaucoup plus étendues qu'elles ne le sont dans cet écrit.[2]

In the second edition of 1664, the "excellent esprit" is identified as "Feu Monsieur Paschal." The first fragment contains a long treatment of two kinds of definitions—"de nom" and "de chose"—and many references to rules of demonstration, but nothing is said about any particular *number* of rules. In the other fragment, much is made again of rules for solid and invariable proofs; Pascal lists eight of them, of which three are not, strictly speaking, essential, which leaves five that are "d'une nécessité absolue";[3] but nothing is said here about the distinction that one may make in the kinds of definitions. One must conclude from the foregoing, I think, (1) that we have in these documents the *écrit* of which the Port-Royalists speak, and (2) that we have a strong precedent for putting them together: men who knew Pascal and what he intended thought of them as somehow unified, as part of the same discussion.[4]

Taken together the two texts do outline and, to some extent, expound a position that is entirely coherent. Both of them are focussed primarily on truth, and on method as the way of stating truth "invincibly" once it is known (rather than as the way of discovering truth). Both of them quickly identify this method with that of geometry, and this step leads in both to a statement of the conditions of proof expressed in terms of definitions, axioms, propositions, and arrangement of these elements. The differences one notes in passing from one document to another are such as to make them complementary rather than opposed. At bottom they represent two angles or approaches to the same situation, the situation in which a truth already possessed by one party (whom I shall call X) is to be stated cogently to someone else (for convenience's sake, Y). The first fragment begins from the point of view of X, moves into a treatment of the quasi-geometrical form in which knowledge must be cast if it is to be demonstrable, and ends just after Pascal has dealt with a hypothetical Y, who cannot see that the infinite divisibility of space or *étendue* is self-evident. The second fragment begins with an analysis of the psychological conditions under which consent to a proposition takes place—in other words, it starts with Y—moves on to a statement of the rules of demonstration, and breaks off in the midst of a defense of this geometrical procedure that a hypothetical X might use. Although these contrasting summaries oversimplify two very dense texts, they will serve to underline the fact that Pascal examines the same process of demonstration or persuasion primarily from the point of view of X in the first fragment, and primarily from that of Y in the second.

As a matter of fact, since the method is the same in either case, whether the aim be demonstration or persuasion, one can only conclude that to demonstrate and to persuade are for Pascal one and the same thing, and that he intends to have geometry—or more precisely, its method or *esprit*—replace rhetoric as the discipline of persuasive speech. Interpersonal discourse has a new and different set of norms by which it will be measured. They are not the norms of logic; that term means first and foremost to Pascal the rules of the syllogism, which he thinks are so much a matter of nature that no one can be ignorant of them (so natural, indeed, that without the art of the geometrician, they are inadequate!); and even in those parts of their treatises where logicians have spoken of the demonstrative rules favored by Pascal, they have failed to see how important they are and how they have consequences for all kinds of orderly thinking. What Pascal does in the second fragment is, I think, to show how the new method dominates the field formerly left to eloquence. The *art de persuader* becomes the *art de démontrer*, and rhetoric apart from geometry is a misleading waste of time. Thus we see exactly what was meant by the word *véritable* in the compliment recorded in the second edition of the *Logique*: "Feu M^r. Pascal qui savait autant de véritable rhétorique, que personne avait jamais su . . . " (p. 341).

On most of the essential points there is no need to add here to what I have already said in the preceding chapter on the difference between logic as the Port-Royalists understood it and the traditional rhetoric. Pascal, too, wishes to remove what would now be called subjective factors from knowing and judging. Instruction easily takes precedence over pleasing and moving as aims of discourse. The rhetoricians prefer to fit their arguments into a loose structure or plan, the parts of which may be moved about or even omitted sometimes. Pascal's idea of order calls for a strict and invariable sequence of proofs where everything (definitions and propositions) depends on everything else and where every element is in its appropriate place, for each piece has the role either of antecedent or consequent with regard to its neighbor. Furthermore, he tends in these fragments to treat language and thought without distinction; he has no interest, if one may judge from his conclusions here, in elocution, that art of adding successive layers of ornament (tropes, figures of speech

113

and thought, rhythms) to the bare expression of truth. In the *Pensées* there is no doubt of his opinion: "Toutes les fausses beautés que nous blâmons en Cicéron ont des admirateurs, et en grand nombre." Or, again, and even more to the point: "L'éloquence est une peinture de la pensée, et ainsi, ceux qui après avoir peint, ajoutent encore, font un tableau au lieu d'un portrait." [5]

In any art or method having to do with language or discourse addressed to an unspecialized listener, the nature of the person spoken to forms an important part of the analysis: he is the one who decides and by deciding fixes the value of the argument. For Quintilian, as for Aristotle, characteristics of age, passions, standing in society, and the like are factors that no orator dares neglect. They affect—in some cases provide—proofs that bring adherence, at least in the particular circumstances and for the time being. More systematic in his procedure, Pascal divides his listener's act of consent into two aspects or, rather, into the acts of two powers: *esprit* and *volonté*. Each of these has its principles or *moteurs*:

> Ceux de l'esprit sont des vérités naturelles et connues à tout le monde, comme que le tout est plus grand que sa partie, outre plusieurs axiomes particuliers que les uns reçoivent et non pas d'autres, mais qui, dès qu'ils sont admis, sont aussi puissants, quoique faux, pour emporter la créance, que les plus véritables. [*Oeuvres,* p. 593.]

There is a similar distinction for the will: certain fixed and natural desires, common to all men, like the desire for happiness, as opposed to variable desires for objects or goods that are in fact effective in their appeal though pernicious (at least when taken as ultimate goods).

Pascal believes that demonstration of the kind described in "De l'esprit géométrique" must attach itself, not to the opinions and desires that vary from person to person, but to *moteurs* invariably and universally present in men. After all, what he wants to bring about through persuasion is a lasting disposition, a permanent conversion; such a commitment calls for an unshakable basis in some truth or aspiration that everyone sees or feels. The orator of Quintilian, attentive to circumstances and *bienséances*, and ready to turn to use the possibilities, temporary or not, in a situation, is likely to be satisfied with any workable starting point; whether that basis will last—because of some universal significance it may have—need not really concern him.

Thus Pascal, like his friends at Port-Royal, felt a tension between genuine rhetoric and that of Cicero and his admirers. It arose from a different attitude toward elocution, the expressive phase of rhetoric, but it goes much deeper than that, to the technique of demonstration and to the mechanism of consent.

We must now attempt to describe in a summary way what might be called the dynamic scheme that underlies Pascal's *art de persuader* or *art de démontrer*. One has only to run through the five rules—eight, in his more fully worked-out version—to locate the elements with which Pascal deals. As I have already said, he takes demonstration to be a process involving definitions, axioms, and propositions. It is the business of the definitions to be explicit and univocal, and of the axioms to be self-evident. In demonstrating, one moves through the steps necessary for seeing the dependence of the propositions on the axioms and definitions. Pascal adds, however, a further and essential step; he indicates what it is but never carries out his intention to treat it fully. "Je passe maintenant à celle [*la règle*, presumably] de l'ordre dans lequel on doit disposer

115

les propositions pour être dans une suite excellente et géométrique . . ." (*Oeuvres*, p. 598). The picture is something like this: definitions and axioms combined with propositions make demonstrations, which are in turn arranged into an order of demonstrations (that is, of propositions with their attendant demonstrations) so that a coherent *suite* is formed. Truths are sequential and systematic; one attains them by composition; they rest on intuitive bases. (Note that in a deductive procedure of this kind one naturally speaks of "truths" rather than of the "truth.")

It is very important to realize that for Pascal this scheme is a mold into which anything truly known will fit. It is dynamic in that it may be extended to all fields of knowledge. In Pascal's mind it assumes the form of an active tendency that seeks further applications. "Il n'y a rien de plus utile et de plus universel," he says (*Oeuvres*, p. 598). I believe that if Pascal had completed these fragments and made of them a truly unified exposition, the result would have been his *Discours de la méthode*. It would have occupied in his thought the moment or stage that precedes certain knowledge of particular matters in just the way that the *Discours* of Descartes precedes his specialized inquiries.

The similarity between the four rules of Descartes and the three phases I have defined above is striking. Descartes' first rule establishes the intuitive bases of knowledge; his second and third rules are focussed on the analysis and solution of problems, that is, with demonstrations; his third and fourth rules, which insist on a smooth passage from the simple to the complex and on the need for completeness, suggest Pascal's interest in an *ordre* that will result in an "excellent and geometrical sequence." But the Cartesian rules are intended both for the discovery and for the exposition of truth—or so they seemed to the logicians of Port-Royal.[6] Pascal's method, as

116

he here describes it, is clearly intended as a way of exposition. The first fragment begins thus:

> I. On peut avoir trois principaux objets dans l'étude de la vérité: l'un de la découvrir quand on la cherche; l'autre de la démontrer quand on la possède; le dernier, de la discerner d'avec le faux quand on l'examine.
> Je ne parle point du premier: je traite particulièrement du second, et il enferme le troisième. [*Oeuvres*, p. 575.]

Moreover, in one way Pascal outdoes Descartes; his terms, definitions, axioms, propositions, demonstrations, and *suites géométriques* are much nearer to geometry than the more generalized language of Descartes: *jugements, difficultés, objets, dénombrements*.

Pascal's scheme or method is first characterized, therefore, by its claim to universality in application. The next thing to note about it is that it alone truly demonstrates.

> Celui [i.e., l'art] de démontrer les vérités déjà trouvées, et de les éclaircir de telle sorte que la preuve en soit invincible, est le seul que je veux donner; et je n'ai pour cela qu'à expliquer la méthode que la géométrie y observe: car elle l'enseigne parfaitement. . . . [*Oeuvres*, p. 576.]

And a few lines below, Pascal adds, still speaking of geometry, ". . . elle seule sait les véritables règles du raisonnement . . ." (*Oeuvres*, p. 576). It alone reasons infallibly; the slight hesitation of the "presque" in the following text is corrected in the rest of the sentence:

> Je veux donc faire entendre ce que c'est que démonstration par l'exemple de celles de géométrie, qui est presque la seule des sciences humaines qui en produise d'infaillibles, parce qu'elle seule observe la véritable méthode, au lieu que toutes les autres sont par une nécessité naturelle dans quelque sorte de confusion que les seules géomètres savent extrêmement connaître. [*Oeuvres*, pp. 576–77.]

117

The claims of uniqueness and of unlimited usefulness that Pascal makes for his favorite technique are certainly strong enough to make us wonder whether he worked from this Euclidean *idée de derrière la tête* in the *Lettres provinciales* and in the *Pensées*. This line of thought leads us away from purely literary considerations, but properly so, I think. Whatever their aesthetic values may be, these works reach out finally beyond themselves. Their underlying principles of construction and order cannot be reduced to poetic forms, since this is literature written in the service of Christian truth as Pascal understands it.

We can say at once that in neither work is he attempting to discover the truth (the first of the *objets* mentioned above), but the essential phrase defining the second aim has a singularly profound echo: " . . . la démontrer quand on la possède." That is, in fact, precisely what Pascal undertakes to do in the *Pensées*. And the second aim includes a third: " . . . la discerner d'avec le faux quand on l'examine," and what is that if not the basic task of the *Lettres provinciales*? In the case of the letters, the correspondence is so close that I should like to point it out in more detail. Pascal's reasoning emerges clearly from this sentence: "Car, si l'on sait la méthode de prouver la vérité, on aura en même temps celle de la discerner, puisqu'en examinant si la preuve qu'on en donne est conforme aux règles qu'on connaît, on saura si elle est exactement démontrée" (*Oeuvres*, p. 575). The *Lettres provinciales* are designed to locate errors, those of Port-Royal's enemies, and they do so in the light of a body of truth that Pascal takes as already known and in the light of a method that he has accepted as valid. In this polemic it is, of course, important to know what the Jesuits have to say on this or that point of doctrine, but it is even more important to examine their way of justifying their views. Since truth depends on method, deficiencies in method become decisive signs of inadequacy or falsity.

What is implied here? Something like this, I believe: Christian truth or truths may be conceived as entering into a sort of *axiomatic system*, characterized by scriptural starting points, by creedal assumptions, by subordinate theorems or positions that come into being as church fathers and theologians apply and elaborate the undisputed *données*, and, finally, by an aspiration to consistency that asserts itself from the outset and makes itself felt through all the later developments. That this or something comparable to it was Pascal's view or criterion can be shown, I think, at many points in the *Lettres provinciales*. What Pascal is doing, as he gives grounds for his own theses or refutes those of his opponents, seems to me to become particularly clear if we refer his procedure to such a model.

This way of looking at the letters obliges us to set aside for a while attention to the things that we usually and rightly admire in them—satire, drama, strong feeling, seemingly effortless control of ideas and means of expression—and to concentrate on the secret working of a factor that, logically speaking, is prior to those qualities. I mean, of course, Pascal's dynamic intuition of method, for this is what generates, as it turns from geometry to the confusion of a theological dispute, the list of topics to be treated; and, at the same time, it defines, broadly and yet decisively, the manner in which they will be treated.

The subject of six of the letters (Nos. 1, 2, 3, 4, 17, 18) is obviously grace, and the sense of that term must be fixed if the discussion is to make any headway. In other words, six letters turn explicitly or implicitly on a problem of definition:

119

hence the usefulness of putting together what Pascal says about this important matter in the two fragments concerning *l'esprit géométrique*. In the first place, he insists on qualities like clarity and intelligibility in definitions. But that is too vague; what he really wants (and he thinks of this as typically and essentially geometrical) is univocity, singleness of meaning for each term, with each meaning made explicit in a single definition, so that whenever in the flow of thought one becomes doubtful or confused, this clarifying formula—agreed upon at the outset—may be substituted for the term. "Voilà une définition géométrique," he writes, after defining an even number as one divisible by two into two equal parts, "parce qu'après avoir clairement désigné une chose, savoir tout nombre divisible en deux également, on lui donne un nom que l'on destitue de tout autre sens, s'il en a, pour lui donner celui de la chose désignée" (*Oeuvres*, p. 577). In a geometrical method one must, therefore, avoid equivocation above all; as *the* sin in logic, it ruins the foundation of any discourse.

What I have said so far suggests such complete liberty on the part of the thinker and places in his hands such complete control of definition that the meanings of words tend to become a matter of private convention. Pascal qualifies this authority. Some terms (as examples: time, movement, number, space) are indefinable; in fact, they become less intelligible when one tries to define them. They have the privilege of being grasped by a *lumière naturelle* common to all men. The resulting clarity surpasses anything that might be achieved even by the geometrician. He would find himself making definitions out of terms that would require further definitions, stated in still other terms, and so on, *ad infinitum*.

On voit assez de là qu'il y a des mots incapables d'être définis; et si la nature n'avait suppléé à ce défaut par une idée pareille qu'elle a donnée à tous les hommes, toutes nos expressions seraient confuses; au lieu qu'on en use avec la même assurance et la même certitude que s'ils étaient expliqués d'une manière parfaitement exempte d'équivoques; parce que la nature nous en a elle-même donné, sans paroles, une intelligence plus nette que celle que l'art nous acquiert par nos explications. [*Oeuvres,* p. 580.]

In any case, where definitions are concerned, Pascal thinks we should seek fixity and perfect intelligibility, either through the help of art (that is, method) or through assent to natural insight.

In what follows I want to stress certain phases of the argument in the first letter, in order to show the role of Pascal's doctrine of definition as an underlying factor in his defense of the Jansenists. It would be possible to make similar points in connection with other letters in this group.

Pascal moves quickly past the *question de fait* (whether the five heretical propositions are in fact in Jansenius' book) to the essential topic, the *question de droit* (whether Arnauld has been understanding the term "grace" improperly). All sides agree that grace confers on the righteous a power that is relevant to and prior to action. However, the Jesuits want to introduce at this point the formula *pouvoir prochain.*

Je chargeai ma mémoire de ce terme, car mon intelligence n'y avait aucune part. Et de peur d'oublier, je fus promptement retrouver mon Janséniste, à qui je dis incontinent, après les premières civilités: Dites–moi, je vous prie, si vous admettez le *pouvoir prochain*? Il se mit à rire et me dit froidement: Dites-moi vous-même en quel sens vous l'entendez, et alors je vous dirai ce que j'en crois. [*Oeuvres,* p. 671.]

The narrator tells him that he understands the term in the sense of the Molinists. But just at this point we note the existence of a confusion that arises because the important term here is used in more than one sense:

Auxquels des Molinistes, me dit-il, me renvoyez-vous?—Je les lui offris tous ensemble, comme ne faisant qu'un seul corps et n'agissant que par un même esprit.

Mais il me dit: vous êtes bien peu instruit. Ils sont si peu dans les mêmes sentiments qu'ils en ont de tout contraires. [*Oeuvres*, p. 671.]

Two things are interesting here. In the first place, the natural assumption of an *esprit géométrique* like that of the inquirer is that the Molinists would as a group be unified in the way that a consistent doctrine would be; they would, in fact, form a group or body because of a body of beliefs or doctrines animated by a single spirit. Pascal writes with an undertone of irony, but he is referring to a genuine ideal of knowledge and understanding. In the second place, the truth of the situation turns out to be just the opposite: a collection of inconsistent and contradictory opinions. Clearly the speakers owe it to themselves and to all interested parties to make explicit the opposed senses and to reduce them to one that is acceptable to both sides if possible.

The narrator goes first to a disciple of M. Le Moine who tells him that, in the case of the *justes, pouvoir prochain* means (1) not to lack anything necessary for action, and then goes on to some Jacobins or neo-Thomists who tell him that having the *pouvoir prochain* means (2) not having all that is required for action (that is, action in accomplishing God's commandments), since a final touch of grace must be added: " . . . il leur faut de plus [aux justes] une grâce efficace qui n'est pas donné à tous, et qui détermine leur volonté à prier; et c'est une hérésie de nier la nécessité de cette grâce pour prier" (*Oeuvres*, p. 673). At once the narrator realizes that the Jansenists are, after all, orthodox, because they hold position (2) and hence the neo-Thomist wing of the Molinists should not be persecuting the Jansenists; it is the allies of the Thomists who are heretical, because they assert position (1). How can these two factions, joined against the Port-Royalists, co-operate when their views are opposed?

The explanation is simple: both groups are out to ruin M. Arnauld; they do not care about consistency of definitions. As the disciple of M. Le Moine says to one of the Thomist fathers who is about to re-affirm view (2): "Voulez-vous recommencer nos brouilleries? ne sommes-nous pas demeurés d'accord de ne point expliquer ce mot de prochain, et de le dire de part et d'autre sans dire ce qu'il signifie? A quoi le Jacobin consentit" (Oeuvres, p. 673–74). The narrator declares the whole affair to be pure chicanery, for there can be no serious discussion without a willingness to consider terms and to come to agreement on the senses they carry. Instead of this logical bona fides, the opponents of M. Arnauld have agreed on nothing except a plot against him. "Pouvoir prochain" is not a very dangerous expression if it consists merely of syllables without sense, though one should not stoop to use a device so unworthy: "Mais ce serait une chose indigne de la Sorbonne et de la théologie d'user de mots équivoques sans les expliquer" (Oeuvres, p. 674). The Molinists are denying the essential nature of words as carriers of meaning; they tell the narrator, that, in order to avoid heresy, one must assert that all just people have the pouvoir prochain, but abstrahendo a sensu Thomistarum et a sensu aliorum theologorum!

The last word is said on the matter when Pascal, through his porte-parole, indicates the way out of the confusion. He has him ask if one finds the expression in Scripture or in the Fathers or in the Councils or in papal usage; and since the answer is "no" each time, we have no need to use it. I believe that Pascal reveals here the key to the problem of definition in religious matters, as he asks: "Quelle nécessité y a-t-il donc de le dire, puisqu'il n'a ni autorité ni aucun sens de lui-même?" (Oeuvres, p. 674). The term might have had a single sense by definition, but that possibility is ruled out by the Molinist disputants; and it might have been similar to words like "time," "movement," "extent"—that is, it might have had a sense in itself, naturally accessible to all, but that possibility is contradicted by the very fact of the dispute. One other possibility remains: the *lumière naturelle* might have given way to supernatural insight coming from authoritative sources, but there is nothing in the genuine supports of the tradition for the term. This is something new. In *De l'esprit géométrique*, Pascal had said nothing about the Bible and the church fathers in connection with definition. From the point of view of function, however, it is clear that the meaning of a word like *grâce* has in theology a place like that of "time" or "motion" in geometry (as Pascal understands that discipline): it is a given from which one works. It must be precisely understood, that is, in a single sense, and for that understanding one looks to divine sources.

The geometric method—or the general approach to knowledge derived from it—draws the attention of a thinker to his definitions, first, and then to the demonstrations by which he validates propositions. In letters Nos. 5 through 10, Pascal shifts, as one might expect, to propositions and proofs. Here he analyzes *la morale des jésuites*, and the key word is *maxime*: over and over again, this or some equivalent expression appears. There can be no doubt that Pascal is now working on a different level, for maxims are principles or propositions having to do with conscience and conduct. The inevitable question soon emerges. What warrant can the Jesuits give for the principles according to which they guide consciences?

We note in the two answers that are given a sharp opposition between a quasi-geometrical guarantee and something much more personal offered by the casuists. As the narrator goes from point to point, the criterion he expects to see and use is that every *maxime* must be drawn from (or at least consistent with) some prior truth taken as axiomatic. To him, certainty and truth are guaranteed only by clear dependence on what has been stated in the Bible, in articles of faith, or in a continuous tradition of the church fathers, popes, and councils. The model of this procedure is one that we have met before: demonstration moves in a tight sequence, starting from things that cannot be doubted and working toward a coherent ensemble of doctrine. However, the narrator comes to the conclusion that the Jesuit fathers have broken with the tradition and have, as a result, removed all possibility of certainty in what they propose as guides in conduct.

> Je ne sais comment vous pouvez faire, quand les Pères de l'Eglise sont contraires au sentiment de quelqu'un de vos casuistes.
> Vous l'entendez bien peu, me dit-il. Les Pères étaient bons pour la morale de leur temps; mais ils sont trop éloignés pour celle du nôtre. Ce ne sont plus eux qui la règlent, ce sont les nouveaux casuistes. [*Oeuvres,* p. 713.]

And Pascal has the "Père" go on to cite the "fameux Père Reginaldus": "Dans les questions de morale, les nouveaux casuistes sont préférables aux anciens Pères, quoiqu'ils fussent plus proches des Apôtres" (*Oeuvres,* p. 713).

Eventually we understand that this rupture has not taken place in an arbitrary way; the trouble simply is that the casuists do not begin with an ideal of certainty and incontradiction as they bring forth their maxims. Theirs is the method of "opinions probables," described at the opening of the fifth letter as "la source et la base de tout ce dérèglement" (*Oeuvres,* p. 706). "C'est le fondement et l'*a b c* de toute notre morale," says the Jesuit father, and he quotes from his authorities:

> Une opinion est appelée probable lorsqu'elle est fondée sur des raisons de quelque considération. D'où il arrive quelquefois qu'un seul docteur fort grave peut rendre une opinion probable.

. . . Car un homme adonné particulièrement à l'étude ne s'attacherait pas à une opinion s'il n'y était attiré par une raison bonne et suffisante. [*Oeuvres*, p. 710.]

The Jesuits find thus their moral principles in the minds of men rather than in the scriptures or in the tradition. From the viewpoint of the narrator and of Pascal, new principles of conduct must be established in the light of things already firmly known, if they are to be certain; but the casuists content themselves with probabilities based on the experiences and reflections of particular men.

The problem of contradiction forces itself upon the narrator:

Qui m'a assuré que dans la liberté que vos docteurs se donnent d'examiner les choses par la raison, ce qui paraîtra sûr à l'un le paraisse à tous les autres? La diversité des jugements est si grande. . . . Vous ne l'entendez pas, dit le Père en m'interrompant; aussi sont-ils fort souvent de différents avis; mais cela n'y fait rien; chacun rend le sien probable et sûr. [*Oeuvres*, p. 711.]

The "Père" is ready for the objection, and we can see why. The presence of contradictions does not shock or offend in the method of the casuists. It will not do in geometry, of course, because geometry requires orderly progress from impersonal and axiomatic truths; it is not a method that encourages or tolerates diversity of opinion; as one of its deepest aspirations, it strives to bring about unanimity.

I do not mean to imply that the Jesuits break completely with proved tradition. When the narrator objects that the Bible, the popes, and the councils, who are in the direct line of the Gospel ("la voie unique de l'Evangile" [*Oeuvres*, p. 714]), cannot be renounced and that they form barriers to the free invention of probable opinions, the Jesuit father undertakes to show that there is no difficulty from that side. In fact, approximately the first half of the sixth letter summarizes precisely those methods by which contradictions between such opinions and dogmatic decisions may be reconciled. There are three techniques: to introduce a distinction in interpreting a word or phrase; if that fails, to appeal to particular circumstances which support the opinion that is or seems to be contradictory; and, as a last resort, to use a subtle new method. The example here is a casuist's rule opposed to a decision in which three popes concur. Nevertheless, one of the Jesuits, Diana, affirms that the dispensation allowed in the rule may be made:

Et comment accorde-t-il cela? lui dis-je. C'est, répliqua le père, par la plus subtile de toutes les nouvelles méthodes, et par le plus fin de la probabilité. . . . C'est que, comme vous le vîtes l'autre jour, l'affirmative et la négative de la plupart des opinions ont chacune quelque probabilité, au jugement de nos docteurs, et assez pour être suivies avec sûreté de conscience [*Oeuvres*, pp. 717–18.]

The formula used for this is the "double probability" of the *pour* and the *contre*: on one of the sides of the argument, we have a decision or principle advanced by the popes, with all the authority inherent in their pronouncement, and, on the other side, the casuist's opinion; but there is no need to decide between them; since both have "probability," one may follow either with security. What happens is not the accommodation of new opinions to authoritative doctrine (which Pascal could not object to); instead, that doctrine is subordinated to the basically skeptical devices of the new probabilities.

There is actually a deeper level of analysis possible here. Why this innovation of method on the part of the casuists? Why adopt a technique of demonstration that produces contradictory opinions as the guiding rules of Christian consciences?

Pascal (in the person of his narrator) is sure that he knows the answer. He imagines a difficulty for the person being guided in the face of the contradictions:

Mais mon Père, lui dis-je, on doit être embarrassé à choisir alors! Point du tout, dit-il, il n'y a qu'à suivre l'avis qui agrée le plus. Eh quoi! si l'autre est plus probable? Il n'importe, me dit-il. Et si l'autre est plus sûr? Il n'importe, me dit encore le Père; le voici bien expliqué. [*Oeuvres,* p. 711.]

He goes on to explain that probability is enough; there is no need to go into questions of degree of probability. The person seeking help may choose, of the *pour* and the *contre,* the more pleasing alternative, even though he does not believe it to be the more probable; and he may do so with complete confidence. A confessor who refused absolution in such a case would be "en état de damnation" (*Oeuvres,* p. 718). The man who consults the casuist determines by a free choice, along the line of least resistance, if he wishes, which of the alternatives is actually true. The priest merely sets up the terms of the choice. That is what damns the method of the casuists in Pascal's eyes: they are not working to produce conversion or moral renewal by means of these probable *maximes.* The effect is to allow the Christian to continue as he is with the added security of a quiet conscience.

But the problem remains: why would the Jesuits permit such relaxation? "Voici quelle est leur pensée" says a Jansenist friend of the narrator:

Ils ont assez bonne opinion d'eux-mêmes pour croire qu'il est utile et comme nécessaire au bien de la religion que leur crédit s'étende partout, et qu'ils gouvernent toutes les consciences. Et parce que les maximes évangéliques et sévères sont propres pour gouverner quelques sortes de personnes, ils s'en servent dans ces occasions où elles leur sont favorables. Mais comme ces mêmes maximes ne s'accordent pas au dessein de la plupart des gens, ils les laissent à l'égard de ceux-là, afin d'avoir de quoi satisfaire tout le monde. [*Oeuvres,* pp. 704-5.]

The casuists thus fall into two groups. There are severe ones for the few who are truly devout, and lax ones (the great majority) for the many Christians who seek laxity. Priests belonging to the second group accept the doctrine of the *opinions probables* as a pragmatic device for gaining public support. Their rules come into being inductively, so to speak, as a result of situations or moral dispositions that exist in fact; they are designed to gain favor and influence rather than to improve lives and souls. The geometrically-minded Christian, like Pascal, starts with the idea that he knows the truth and that he is going to demonstrate it to someone who does not yet know that truth. The casuist of the more typical kind talks or behaves as if the customer were always right, when his real function is to convince himself first of the truth of his maxims and then to show them, with the force of proof behind them, to the people he advises: this is something quite different from offering two or more contrasting formulas to someone who will make up his mind according to his own disposition. Such "truths" arise out of particular circumstances and personal relationships. Their value is determined by what is applicable and effective or what is thought to be probably so.

The *esprit de géométrie* leads one to be especially careful about terms or definitions, about the status of propositions, and about the sequence or order of propositions. We have now seen a reflection of the first two of these topics in several of the letters. What of the concept of an ensemble of doctrine? Does it have a role in the work? I think that the answer must be yes; and the unity in question is easily shown if one follows out two lines of thought, basing the first on the idea of historical sequence and the second on that of systematic wholeness or consistency, although both turn out to be essentially the same thing.

As Pascal approaches his polemic tasks in the *Provinciales*,

as he distinguishes the true from the false—one of the uses of
the geometrical method, it will be recalled—a continuous
historical account is present in his mind. He expresses it or
indicates it most simply when he refers to "l'écriture et la
tradition de l'Eglise" (*Oeuvres*, p. 709). The latter obviously
depends on the former and grows out of it in an organic way.
Pascal sometimes analyzes further each of these two great
factors: The Bible may appear as containing a sequence from
the patriarchs to the prophets to Christ to St. Paul and the
apostles; and the succeeding part of the story may be traced in
links provided by the church fathers (with special mention for
St. Augustine and for the last of the fathers, St. Bernard), by
St. Thomas, and, finally, by the judgments of popes and councils (see, e.g., *Oeuvres*, p. 683). At any point along this line,
Pascal may point out conflicts involving the "new" Thomists
and the casuists. We may have the Gospel versus the casuists
(p. 772), or the fathers versus the casuists (p. 713), or St.
Paul versus the casuists (p. 777); and sometimes the line as a
whole stands against them, as when one tries by various devices to make certain *opinions probables* acceptable. Without
attempting anything like a detailed history of beliefs—to do
so would spoil the plan of the letters and lose readers as well
—Pascal gives us to understand that an unbroken sequence
does exist in the background of the present dispute.

In the first letter and in the seventeenth and eighteenth,
that is, at the beginning and at the end of the *Provinciales*,
Pascal insists on the difference between a *question de fait*
and a *question de droit ou de foi*. The second line of thought
that I have proposed, since it turns on coherence rather than
on historical elaboration, is closely tied to this distinction.
The *question de droit ou de foi* belongs, I believe, on the
plane of the geometrical spirit, of that tendency that assumes
and provides a structure into which knowledge must fit. And
so this overarching antithesis, which to my mind serves as the

key to the whole undertaking of the *Provinciales,* takes on its typically Pascalian nuance in the light of his fondness for the *esprit géométrique. A question de fait* has nothing to do with geometry; it asks, did *X* say what he is alleged to have said? The question and the answer to it involve the senses and, insofar as method is concerned, call for canons based on the conditions of accurate observation. A *question de droit,* however, is quite independent of operations of sense; it asks, does what *X* said or is alleged to have said square with what we already know to be true?

In letters Nos. 1, 2, 3, 4, 17 and 18, where the discussions turn on opposed notions of *grâce* and its effects, and in letters Nos. 5, 6, 7, 8, 9 and 10, where Pascal attacks the moral maxims of the Jesuits, he places himself on the terrain of *droit* or *foi:* he is asserting the incompatibility between what they say and what must be taken as truth, given the Bible and the Christian tradition. Even letter No. 11, in which he defends irony and satire as justifiable in his campaign, contains an appeal to orthodox sources:

Ne prétendez pas, mes Pères, de faire accroire au monde que ce soit une chose indigne d'un Chrétien de traiter les erreurs avec moquerie, puisqu'il est aisé de faire connaître à ceux qui ne le sauraient pas que cette pratique est juste, qu'elle est commune aux Pères de l'Eglise, et qu'elle est autorisée par l'Ecriture, par l'exemple des plus grands saints, et par celui de Dieu même. [*Oeuvres,* p. 780.]

The remaining letters (Nos. 12, 13, 14, 15, 16) involve mainly *questions de fait:* did particular casuists and others make the statements and argue for the principles that Pascal had criticized in letters Nos. 5 through 10?

When Pascal returns, in the last two complete letters, to the five propositions and to the issue of heresy, he uses both arguments *de facto* and arguments *de jure.* In terms of the former he challenges once again Père Annat to locate verbatim the propositions in Jansenius' book. But this challenge, which Pascal takes as unanswerable, is less decisive than the turn he gives to the controversy by reasoning in the perspective *de jure*. If the propositions are in the book and have the sense condemned by the Jesuits (that is, the "sens de Calvin"), all parties to the dispute, Port-Royalists as well as everyone else, reject them as inconsistent with sound doctrine concerning grace and the freedom of will to resist it. As soon as he realized, says Pascal, that the dispute was not about possibly heretical tenets, he began to lose interest in it:

Dès lors votre dispute commença à me devenir indifférente. Quand je croyais que vous disputiez de la vérité ou de la fausseté des propositions, je vous écoutais avec attention; car cela touchait la foi: mais quand je vis que vous ne disputiez plus que pour savoir si elles étaient *mot à mot* dans Jansenius ou non, comme la religion n'était plus intéressée, je ne m'y intéressai plus aussi. [*Oeuvres*, p. 872.]

Pascal does not give up on the factual question; he thinks that it is possible to disagree—in the line of fact—on what the "sens de Jansenius" is and that it is possible, consequently, to understand him in a way that does not contradict in the least the position of St. Augustine and St. Thomas on grace and its operation. Naturally this is the way in which Pascal and those with whom he sympathizes do understand Jansenius. It is nonetheless true that the discussion in the letters does not move toward an effort to state differing interpretations of what Jansenius said in fact; it suffices that all hands agree on the central doctrines. Pacal emphasizes one question only: whether or not the propositions in dispute are equivalent to ones that are already received as valid within the system of beliefs.

As expressed in the eighteenth letter, Pascal's views include in reality a third sort of question. Starting with a reference to questions of fact, he goes on to show the rest of his hand:

D'où apprendrons-nous donc la vérité des faits? Ce sera des yeux, mon Père, qui en sont les légitimes juges, comme la raison l'est des choses naturelles et intelligibles, et la foi des choses surnaturelles et révélées. Car, puisque vous m'y obligez, mon Père, je vous dirai que, selon les sentiments de deux des plus grands docteurs de l'Eglise, saint Augustin et St. Thomas, ces trois principes de nos connaissances, les sens, la raison et la foi, ont chacun leurs objets séparés, et leur certitude dans cette étendue. [*Oeuvres*, p. 897.]

The statement of the relations of these *étendues* and principles, as they emerge in the *Provinciales*, will serve to summarize the main points of my analysis. *Questions de fait* have to be judged in the light of sense experience: for example, did Jansenius actually affirm the five propositions in so many words, *iisdem verbis*, so that all may *see* the truth of the allegations? *Questions de foi* have to be decided, not by reference to sensation—although Pascal points out that by the principle of *fides ex auditu*, faith is based on sense experience in an important sense—but in the light of Scripture and of decisions handed down by the Church. The intermediate order of *raison* seems to have no relevance to the problems of the *Provinciales*, and we know from the famous passage in the *Pensées* on the three orders, which corresponds so closely to what Pascal says in this eighteenth letter, that the realms of *corps*, *esprit*, and *charité* are infinitely distant from one another. And yet, is it not clear that Pascal has transposed the geometrical ideal and technique into the uppermost of his orders? When the time comes for faith to examine and justify itself, and to assert itself against the intrusion of error, it reverts for its mode of analysis and for its criterion of validity to the method of reason. Pascal has chosen to deal with Jesuits and other opponents of Port-Royal (1) by asking for definitions with clear and single meanings; (2) by isolating statements, maxims, and propositions in the moral theory of the Jesuits and in the views of Jansenius; and (3) by sketching a line of theological demonstrations that arise from axiomatic beginnings and eventually group themselves into a system, such being the aim toward which faith, like geometry, inevitably moves.

Perhaps the fairest way to judge what has happened is to say, not that Pascal has applied the method of geometry to a religious controversy, but something subtler. I mean, that geometry itself is merely the application of a general methodological insight; its method is the particular technique inspired by that insight when someone makes it relevant to *mouvement, nombre, espace, temps;* and thus the appearance of "geometrical" schemes in the *Lettres provinciales,* rather than being a transfer, is, instead, another incarnation of a tendency that stands above any one of its scientific or polemic uses.

Such transposition or re-use is not feasible when the character of the reader changes, as it does in a very significant way when Pascal begins to plan his apology of the Christian religion and to write the *Pensées.* For him the two factors of method and audience vary together; changes in one imply changes in the other. The *Provinciales* owe an important part of their persuasiveness to the fact that the reader, the "provincial," and those like him, are men of good sense, of good senses, and of faith (to mention all three of the means to knowledge) and the quasi-geometrical substructure of the work is well attuned to the members of such an audience. They share the premises from which Pascal begins; he is showing them how what they already know and accept makes possible, when it is used in an orderly manner, the detection of error and malice in the doctrines and attitudes held by the enemies of Port-Royal. It is not for such believers that he writes in the *Pensées*. There he wishes to attract the attention of readers who feel indifferent to religion or even hostile to it.

His problem is, as usual, to find something on which to build. He cannot start with religious beliefs, but he must locate something equally firm; and we know that he eventually finds it in the instabilities and contradictions of human nature, in the everlasting conflict between what man wants and thinks he is entitled to—truth and happiness—and what he can actually have. These contradictions he cannot eliminate by a drive toward simplicity and faultless demonstrations, in other words, by applying the genius of the geometrical method. And so he adopts a procedure that is Augustinian (eventually Platonic) in origin, the method of dialectical harmonization. The conflicts that lead to the logical style of the *Provinciales* come mainly from errors of definition and reasoning and represent impurities in a body of doctrine and practice; hence they may be corrected by the application of the *esprit de géométrie*. The *Pensées* begin with something more fundamental; human nature in its fallen state. The contradictions found there do not arise from the misuse of words and from non sequiturs in reasoning. They inhere in a subject and they require for their proper treatment a technique that will, in its first phase, make the contrarieties pitilessly clear and then, in its second phase, show how one may harmonize the opposed traits or tendencies by subordinating them to God. I have shown elsewhere [7] that one may classify many of the *Pensées* under headings corresponding either to those two phases or to aspects of them: the recognition of psychological and moral conflicts; the emphasis on their real or "existential" character; the resulting perplexity as one faces them; the search for a solution; the discovery of the simultaneous truth of the opposites when a comprehensive principle harmonizes them; the self-validating feature of the whole process, since it results in unity (an important sign of truth) and since those who contest it may be relegated to the stage that precedes the dialectical resolution.

I do not wish to separate entirely the working of the *esprit de géométrie* and that of the dialectical spirit in Pascal's thought. Remnants of the one turn up in the other, as Pascal modulates from one perspective to the other. In the first section of "De l'esprit géométrique," where he illustrates the method of geometry by going briefly into the *notions premières* of that science, he lists, as the common properties of things, movement, number, and space or extent. Actually there is a scriptural source for these terms, and Pascal cites it: "Deus fecit omnia in pondere, in numero et in mensura" (Sap., XI, 21). These three properties serve respectively as starting points for the three branches of *géométrie* (in its generic sense) which are *mécanique, arithmétique,* and *géométrie* (in its specific sense).

> Ainsi il y a des propriétés communes à toutes choses, dont la connaissance ouvre l'esprit aux plus grandes merveilles de la nature.
> La principale comprend les deux infinités qui se rencontrent dans toutes: l'une de grandeur, l'autre de petitesse. [*Oeuvres*, p. 583–84.]

As a consequence, any movement, number or space or time (associated with movement by Pascal), is always situated between something quantitatively larger and something quantitatively smaller, and one is ultimately justified in saying that " . . . ils se soutiennent tous entre le néant et l'infini" (*Oeuvres*, p. 584).

> Mais ceux qui verront clairement ces vérités pourront admirer la grandeur et la puissance de la nature dans cette double infinité qui nous environne de toutes parts, et apprendre par cette considération merveilleuse à se connaître eux-mêmes, en se regardant

placés entre une infinité et un néant d'étendue, entre une infinité et un néant de nombre, entre une infinité et un néant de mouvement, entre une infinité et un néant de temps. Sur quoi on peut apprendre à s'estimer à son juste prix, et former des réflexions qui valent mieux que tout le reste de la géométrie même. [*Oeuvres,* p. 591.]

This is but a step from the great passages on the "Disproportion de l'homme" of the *Pensées.* There man stands as a whole, as a colossus, in respect to the small infinite and as a *néant* in respect to the opposed infinite; and there the physical paradox opens up an unending series of simultaneously present contraries in man. We recognize in him knowledge of middle things but not of extremes, that is, knowledge that is also ignorance; spirit that is attached to body; aspirations to truth and felicity attached to knowing powers that are inadequate and objects of desire that are elusive; and so on, as we move through the dialectical paths of the *Pensées.*

If we turn now to the *Pensées* for echoes and vestiges of the geometrical mind, we first recognize that Pascal foresees there two main possibilities, after he has brought about a favorable disposition in his reader by argumentation (such as that of the *pari*). One may become the Christian who knows and judges by the heart or one may in addition know by reasoning, with the aid of prophecies and proofs. In either case one is persuaded:

Ceux que nous voyons chrétiens sans la connaissance des prophéties et des preuves ne laissent pas d'en juger aussi bien que ceux qui ont cette connaissance. Ils en jugent par le coeur comme les autres en jugent par l'esprit. C'est Dieu qui les incline à croire et ainsi ils sont très efficacement persuadés. [*Oeuvres,* pp. 1344–45.]

The reappearance of the word *preuves* is significant; it occurs many times, of course, in "De l'esprit géométrique." We must note, however, its ambiguity in the *Pensées:*

137

Car il ne faut pas se méconnaître: nous sommes automate autant qu'esprit; et de là vient que l'instrument par lequel la persuasion se fait n'est pas la seule démonstration. Combien y a-t-il peu de choses démontrées! Les preuves ne convainquent que l'esprit. La coutume fait nos preuves les plus fortes et les plus crues; elle incline l'automate, qui entraîne l'esprit sans qu'il y pense. [*Oeuvres*, p. 1219.]

Of the two sorts of proofs—reasons and custom or habit—the former are provided for, even though they have an inferior place in Pascal's apologetics. That they are associated with geometry is shown by the return of the notion of demonstration. It is the same with other elements of the earlier and more technical vocabulary. After the passage cited above, "Ceux que nous voyons chrétiens . . . , " Pascal first wrote, and then crossed out, a few lines in defense of those who know by and are guided by the heart. He thinks of an objection to this effect, that heretics and *infidèles* go astray precisely because their faith centers in the heart; here is his answer:

> . . . Je réponds à cela que nous avons des preuves . . . et que les infidèles n'ont aucune preuve de ce qu'ils disent et ainsi nos *propositions* étant semblables dans les *termes* elles diffèrent en ce que l'une est sans aucune preuve et l'autre très solidement prouvée.[8]

Pascal's attitude toward the infidels and the heretics reminds us of the one he assumes toward his opponents in the *Provinciales:* to combat error he instinctively falls back on terms and propositions duly expressed and ordered.

In an interesting fragment he ties the idea of proof to twelve subordinate topics:

PREUVE. — 1 ° La religion chrétienne, par son établissement: par elle-même établie si fortement, si doucement, étant si contraire à la nature. — 2 ° La sainteté, la hauteur et l'humilité d'une âme chrétienne. — 3 ° Les merveilles de l'Ecriture sainte.

— 4 ° Jésus-Christ en particulier. — 5 ° Les apôtres en particulier. — 6 ° Moïse et les prophètes en particulier. — 7 ° Le peuple juif. — 8 ° Les prophéties. — 9 ° La perpétuité: nulle religion n'a la perpétuité. — 10 ° La doctrine, qui rend raison de tout. — 11 ° La sainteté de cette loi. — 21 ° Par la conduite du monde. [*Oeuvres*, p. 1228.]

No one can say exactly what Pascal would have done with this list of topics had he finished the project. What he did do, for example, in connection with the history of the Jews, prophecies, and the question of *perpétuité* in other fragments makes it plausible for one to conclude that each of these headings implied in his mind a proposition or a small group of propositions which he intended to prove. The list suggests, thus, a series—or perhaps a vaguer word would be safer here—a group of demonstrations. It reminds us of that order (in Pascal's terms, " . . . l'ordre dans lequel on doit disposer les proposition pour être dans une suite excellente et géométrique," *Oeuvres*, p. 598) toward which the geometrical spirit aspires in its second phase, after particular points have been established. In any case, the *preuve* resulting from this twelve-fold demonstration has for him a definite unity. He sees it as a whole that carries his reader with certainty to his general conclusion:

Il est indubitable qu'après cela on ne doit pas refuser, en considérant ce que c'est que la vie, et que cette religion, de suivre l'inclination de la suivre, si elle nous vient dans le coeur; et il est certain qu'il n'y a nul lieu de se moquer de ceux qui la suivent. [*Oeuvres*, pp. 1228–29.]

It would be wrong, therefore, to think of geometry and dialectic as mutually exclusive in Pascal's mind. One leads to the other, as when the properties of things bring us to the play of the infinities; and one makes use of the other, as when we see that the Christian religion, though a matter of conversion and of the heart at first, may become proven knowledge. Nevertheless, our final statement must be, I think, that each of these *esprits* has its own framework and technique in science and in morality. We can see one art of persuasion first treated theoretically in the unfinished texts with which we began and then put to practical use in the *Lettres provinciales;* and we can see in the *Pensées* how a different problem, aim, and audience led Pascal to develop another way to the truth.

1. For details concerning the manuscripts, see *Oeuvres complètes,* ed. Léon Brunschvicg *et al.* ("Grands Ecrivains de la France" [Paris, 1914]), 231 ff., and *Oeuvres complètes,* ed. Jacques Chevalier ("Bibliothèque de la Pléiade" [Paris, 1954]), p. 575.

2. See Brunschvicg, *Oeuvres,* IX, 231, where this paragraph is reprinted from the *Logique.*

3. Page 597 in the Chevalier edition (see note 1, above). All further quotations from Pascal cited in this chapter are taken from this edition.

4. I should also mention, as part of the history of the association of these texts, that they were together in a manuscript once in the possession of Sainte-Beuve, used by Faugère, but now lost.

5. Pages 1096 and 1099, respectively; fragments 33 and 48. The analogy drawn between thought and ornamented expression, on one side, and portraits and pictures, on the other, reminds one of the relation of man to author in another fragment: "Quand on voit le style naturel, on est tout étonné et ravi, car on s'attendait à voir un auteur, et on trouve un homme" (p. 1096. no. 36). The theme of the author as decorator (stylistically speaking) is further emphasized elsewhere: "Tout ce qui n'est que pour l'auteur ne vaut rien. *Ambitiosa recidet ornamenta*" (p. 1096, no. 34). That snippet from Horace is an ornament of sorts!

6. See the *Logique,* IVᵉ partie, chap. ii.

7. In my essay "Conflict and Resolution in Pascal's *Pensées,*" *Romanic Review,* XLIX, No. 1 (February, 1958), 12–24.

8. *Pensées,* ed. L. Lafuma (Paris, 1951), I, 222 (italics added).

Chapter VI

Three Conceptions of the Audience

𝔍T was the habit of Corneille and Racine to provide discourses, epistles, prefaces, or other supporting statements when they presented their plays to the public in printed form. Molière was less systematic, but from him we have the *Critique de l'Ecole des femmes, L'Impromptu de Versailles,* and the substantial documents accompanying *Tartuffe.* One approaches these texts with the hope that they will give something like a direct look at the values and methods that guided the three dramatists. One leaves them enlightened, surely, but disappointed.

We do get from Racine's prefaces a sense of the curve described by his genius: the growing awareness and control of his form, beautifully realized in *Bérénice* and *Andromaque;* the perfecting of it in *Phèdre;* then, after a silence, the return with a new vision in *Esther* and *Athalie.* In his two critical plays Molière speaks briefly (and for a while in person) of his kind of comedy. Corneille's discourses, *examens,* and prefaces are the most satisfying of all from the point of view of dramatic theory, because of their scope and precision. To have a dramatist of his stature say so carefully what his principles are—or rather, as in the *Discours* and *Examens,* what they have become for the 1660 edition of his works—is a rare piece of good luck. Still, these prefaces and assorted papers leave much of our curiosity unsatisfied. Corneille takes for granted his distinctive moral universe of dilemmas, choices, and tests, since all that falls under the heading of *moeurs* and therefore lies outside of poetic art as he conceives it; Racine says almost nothing about style; and Molière's two little comedies are fascinating and tantalizing by turns, since they give so much space to satirical commonplaces and to the problem of meeting the king's deadline that what happens in between, that is, between the discussion of general ideas and a finished comedy, eludes us. But Corneille's ethic, Racine's expression, and Molière's gift of comic invention are to us matters of first importance, and we find ourselves wishing that they had had more to say on those subjects.

The difficulty comes, of course, from the fact that we are inclined to make these documents do more than they are intended to do. With the possible exception of the *Discours* of Corneille—and even there the case is not simple—none of them is, in essence, designed to introduce us to the poetics of the author; they give us rather his reaction to his audience's reaction. Corneille, Racine, and Molière write what they consider to be suitable prefaces to the printed versions of works that have already been performed and commented on; as reactions to reactions they have, therefore, the traits of arguments *ad hoc* rather than of theoretic statements.

I should like to propose, then, that we approach these arguments from another direction. Instead of asking what they *say* on the subject of poetic theory, let us concentrate on what they *signify,* that is, on what they tell us about the typical relationship between dramatic poets and their audiences in the seventeenth century, and especially on what they tell us about the way in which each of the dramatists, having accepted as a matter of course the typical relationship, goes on to refine it, to imagine in his own fashion his audience and to dispose himself toward it.

It is obvious that the dramatic literature of any period tends, by its nature, to be dependent on audience support. In the seventeenth century, however, this condition is reinforced by special economic and social factors, with the result that the audience has both in theory and in fact a decisive role in the creation of literature. In outline the view from which I start is that Corneille, Racine, and Molière find and see themselves engaged in literary transactions (that word being taken in its etymological sense) that have three aspects or phases: poet, work, and spectator. These three aspects are, in fact, links in a causal chain; what the poet does in his creative activity is the cause of the work, and the work, when performed, becomes in turn the cause of an experience in the spectator's senses, heart, and mind. It is this experience or the quality of it that determines more than anything else the value that is attached to the work and to the art of the poet. In short, by accepting the basic set of human and artistic factors in the relationship I have defined, Corneille, Racine, and Molière accept a rhetorical approach to literature in general and to drama in particular.

In any such set of complicated factors in which one element is dominant, as the audience is here, we expect a natural tendency toward some sort of balance, toward some limitation of the dominant principle. Great poets are not going to leave all decisions having to do with the value of their works up to their audiences. The prefaces, discourses, and playlets studied here are, for the most part, attempts on the part of the dramatists to achieve such a balance. As they explain and defend themselves, they reveal characteristic and personal ways of coming to terms with a privileged public always in danger of slipping into arbitrary judgments. Actually there are only two main lines of appeal open to any dramatist who has adopted the notion of literature as a kind of rhetorical activity. (1) He may invent special qualifications which must be present in his audience before he will abide by its ver-

dicts, distinguishing thus between those who are really qualified and those who, because of ignorance or hostility, need
not be taken seriously. Or, (2) he may shift the grounds of
the argument, so that artistic principles come to the fore;
instead of making distinctions in his audience or appealing
to some audience that he wishes he had, he justifies his work
by showing that what he has done is right, poetically speaking. (Of course, there remains a third possibility, which is
to combine in varying proportions these two, so that at times
the poet defends himself on grounds that are basically moral or
psychological and at other times on premises that are basically
technical or artistic.) The interesting thing is to see how
each of the three poets has, by temperament and by choice,
his favorite among these possibilities and his own way of
working with it.

Corneille wrote three *Discours* on dramatic poetry, one for
each volume of the first collected edition of his works. As
these essays make clear, he has an *abstract* idea of his audience that guides him in the process of creation. Although,
as we shall see, the *actual* audience is the one that means
most to him, the abstract one gives us a convenient approach
to the other.

In the first place, then, Corneille counts on the presence
of certain human traits in his or in any public. His discussion of pity and fear, of the incidents that arouse those emotions, of the heroes who will arouse the admiration which
he thinks of as his contribution to the list of possible dramatic
effects, in fact his whole treatment of the topic of the effects
that are sought by serious drama is determined by reference
to human values and sensibilities that are essentially the same
everywhere and at all times. The same idea of an abstract

or typical audience (as opposed to a particular one) underlies his argument when he sets forth in what ways dramatic
poems make us better. We are improved by the maxims they
contain, by the examples of vices and virtues they offer, with
the good and bad fates that follow from them, and by the
purgations that such poems bring about; and on all of these
points, it is evident that Corneille does not see the *utilité* of
dramatic poems as something tailored uniquely to the character of his seventeenth-century audiences; it has a universal
validity.

In the second place, however, as important and fundamental as this concept is, it is overlaid with something more
particular that definitely varies according to place and time.
One must, for example, take into account the difference between French spectators and the ancients. Corneille has just
expressed his disagreement with Aristotle, who condemns
the fourth of a list of types of tragic situations and actions.
This fourth kind, in which characters who know what they
want to do, undertake to do it, and then fail to accomplish
the act, is said by Aristotle to have nothing tragic about it.

Il y a grande apparence que ce qu'a dit ce philosophe de ces
divers degrés de perfection pour la tragédie avait une entière
justesse de son temps, et en la présence de ses compatriotes . . .
mais aussi je ne puis m'empêcher de dire que le goût de notre
siècle n'est point celui du sien sur cette préférence d'une espèce
à l'autre, ou du moins que ce qui plaisait au dernier point à ses
Athéniens ne plaît pas également à nos Français. . . .[1]

The "Examen du *Cid*," written at about the same time, introduces other and even finer distinctions. Corneille explains
that he has been obliged to make changes in his source. As
he conceives his subject, he may not allow Rodrigue to marry
Chimène in the play; he must content himself with saving
his hero. The marriage, he says,

145

. . . est historique, et a plu en son temps; mais bien sûrement il déplairait au nôtre; et j'ai peine à voir que Chimène y consente chez l'auteur espagnol, bien qu'il donne plus de trois ans de durée à la comédie qu'il en a faite.[2]

And so one cannot follow blindly Greek or Spanish taste and expect to please French audiences.

Another interesting idea is expressed in this same "Examen": that French taste itself varies from one time to another. Corneille judges quite severely two scenes, the one in which Rodrigue offers his sword to Chimène in order that she may kill him and avenge her father's death and the later one in which he says that his "fidèle ardeur" takes away his desire to defend himself in the duel with Don Sanche.

Ces beautés étaient de mise en ce temps-là, et ne le seraient pas en celui-ci. La première est dans l'original espagnol, et l'autre est tirée sur ce modèle. Toutes les deux ont fait leur effet en ma faveur; mais je ferais scrupule d'en étaler de pareilles à l'avenir sur notre théâtre. [III, 95.]

This judgment appeared first in the edition of 1660, some twenty-four years after the first performances of Le Cid. But Corneille does not content himself with deploring the past and resolving to do something else in the future. For this edition he made many changes of diction and style in his original texts, so many, in fact, that it is a notable monument to the purification of taste through which he had himself lived. This moral and literary evolution explains, as a recent study has shown,[3] a number of revisions in the ending of Le Cid.

We see an indirect indication of this theme of the changing audience in Corneille's clear and explicit desire to innovate. For him it is not enough to stay in the old paths, in the *chemins battus*. What has pleased once is a matter of history; after being satisfied with one kind of fare, the taste of the audience will surely turn to something else. Again and again, from *Mélite* onward, we find mentions of this quest for novelty. Here is a typical example, from the *dédicace* of *Don Sanche*:

Voici un poème d'une espèce nouvelle, et qui n'a point d'exemple chez les anciens. Vous connaissez l'humeur de nos Français; ils aiment la nouveauté; et je hasarde non *tam meliora quam nova*, sur l'espérance de les mieux divertir. [V, 404.]

Then support from the ancients is furnished by Horace's comments on Greek audiences and Roman poets, the former " . . . apud quos / Illecebris erat et grata novitate morandus / Spectator. . . . " ("Among whom the spectator had to be held by charms and pleasing novelty.") And the latter

Vel qui praetextas, vel qui docuere togatas / Nec minimum meruere decus vestigia Graeca / Ausi deserere. . . . [*Ars poetica*, 223–24, 286–88.]

("Who, as authors of both tragedies and comedies, dared to forsake the footsteps of Greece: that was not the least of their merits.")

The other side of the coin, the dark side corresponding to this responsiveness to changing public taste, turns up at a critical point in Corneille's career; I mean, when he concludes after the failure of *Pertharite* (1652) that he is no longer in touch with the public. One cannot read the lines without emotion:

La mauvaise réception que le public a faite à cet ouvrage m'avertit qu'il est temps que je sonne la retraite. . . . Il vaut mieux que je prenne congé de moi-même que d'attendre qu'on me le donne tout à fait; et il est juste qu'après vingt années de travail, je commence à m'apercevoir que je deviens trop vieux pour être encore à la mode. [VI, 5.]

If such is the basic conception that Corneille has of his audience—that it shares some traits with all audiences, but above all else is particular and changing—what is his *attitude* toward it? The essence of his attitude shows through the lines I have just quoted. He accepts the reactions of his public almost without question. From the start of his career as a dramatist, he gives the trump cards, so to speak, to the spectators, because he takes *plaire* as the first principle of dramatic art; and, after that, there is little one may do other than assent to their decisions; for it is useless to try to demonstrate to an audience that it did, against its own sentiments, enjoy a performance or to argue that it should have done so. In 1637, he composed for publication, along with the text of *La Suivante,* an epistle to M. ***, which was left anonymous, perhaps because of the boldness of the reflections that Corneille wished to present. We find in it a passage that sums up the view to which he returns many times in succeeding prefaces:

Cependant mon avis est celui de Térence: puisque nous faisons des poèmes pour être représentés, notre premier but doit être de plaire à la cour et au peuple, et d'attirer un grand monde à leurs représentations. [II, 119.][4]

Then Corneille mentions the rules, which come unmistakably in second place:

Il faut, s'il se peut, y ajouter les règles, afin de ne déplaire pas aux savants, et recevoir un applaudissement universel; mais surtout gagnons la voix publique. . . . " [II, 119-20.]

Some spectators and critics insist on conformity to rules as the basis of excellence in drama but not Corneille: public approval—the sign that a play has pleased—is to him the indispensable requirement.

Nowhere does he make this clearer than in the *examen*

of *Le Cid*. He interprets its success in English, Italian, and Flemish versions (as well as in French) as decisive justification for the liberties he had taken with the rules (although he contends elsewhere that his play is basically regular). In another *examen*, that of *Andromède*, he takes a step even further in the direction of nonconformity, as he justifies the use of *stances*, irregular lines, and rhymes as a means of arriving at the end of the art. Of course, Corneille is perfectly willing to congratulate himself on a coincidence of dramatic success and observance of rules, as in the cases of *Cinna* and *Polyeucte*; but where there is a conflict between regularity and popularity, his empiricism and his taste for what works in the theater assert themselves. And for the last words to the reader in the short introduction to *Suréna*, his last play, he writes: "Vous en jugerez."

One may say that it is easy for a writer like Corneille, who usually has the public on his side, to accept its judgments. The fact is that even when one of his works fails— in the popular sense—he blames himself, not the audience. The *Suite du menteur*, for example, did not succeed so well as the play to which it formed a sequel, although Corneille judged it, he says in the epistle, to have more "beaux sentiments" and "beaux vers":

Ce n'est pas que j'en veuille accuser ni le défaut des acteurs, ni le mauvais jugement du peuple: la faute en est tout à moi, qui devais mieux prendre mes mesures, et choisir des sujets plus répondants au goût de mon auditoire. [IV, 279.]

Or, again, apropos of *Théodore*:

. . . Sa représentation n'a pas eu grand éclat; et quoique beaucoup en attribuent la cause à diverses conjonctures qui pourraient me justifier aucunement, pour moi je ne m'en veux prendre qu'à ses défauts, et la tiens mal faite, puisqu'elle a été mal suivie. J'aurais tort de m'opposer au jugement du public. . . . [V, 8.]

Here he does allow himself a pointed remark about taste. The theme of prostitution, unavoidable in his subject, had proved a stumbling block for his public. The moral purity of the contemporary theater is thus demonstrated, he concludes, since a story greatly appreciated in the version that St. Ambrose gives in his *De virginibus* is too licentious for a French audience in 1645.

Corneille acquiesces if the play does not win popular favor; and by "popular" I mean to include a wide range from the humblest spectators to members of the court and to exclude critics who reason from theory and from learning. This is, in fact, the only significant distinction that he sees in his public: the many versus the erudite few. If he makes no serious effort to appeal adverse judgments from the former, he does respond, with tact, firmness, and ingenuity, to the opinions of the latter. He reminds them that they speak usually as grammarians and philosophers rather than as poets and that they are free to try to do better than he has done. Then he goes out to meet them on their own ground with arms of their choice. If they will judge his plays according to the rules, he intends to have his say in those terms. His discourses and his *examens* are, in a way, formal claims to the right of the poet to analyze and defend his works in the perspective of art; and in spite of a certain diffidence that he shows from time to time, he appears determined to outthink the critical specialists. In the first discourse, he goes right to the point, which is for him their inadequate grasp of the nature of poetic principles. His own secret lies in his relatively free attitude toward the regulation of art by theory. To the dogmatist who likes to ask of any work whether it observes the rules and imitates the ancients, Corneille slyly quotes ancients who see a place for innovation; he recalls Horace's praise for poets of his own time: "Nec minimum meruere decus, vestigia Graeca/ Ausi deserere," and then the scornful exclamation: "O imitatores, servum pecus,"[5] and concludes by translating from the *Annals* of Tacitus (Bk. XI, chap. xxiv):

Ce qui nous sert maintenant d'exemple, dit Tacite, a été autrefois sans exemple, et ce que nous faisons sans exemple en pourra servir un jour. [I, 25.]

This liberal attitude is eventually justified by what happens in fact or practice. For example, although the perfection of tragedy consists, according to the usual formula, in the arousal of pity and fear for the protagonist, Corneille proposes *Polyeucte* as a work that excites pity without fear and still succeeds.

Cela posé, trouvons quelque modération à la rigueur de ces règles du philosophe, ou du moins quelque favorable interprétation, pour n'être pas obligés de condamner beaucoup de poèmes que nous avons vu réussir sur nos théâtres. [I, 63.]

He wants his critics to know that he, too, knows something about regularity and irregularity and how those terms have to be kept flexible and in harmony with search and novelty and respect for experience. His choice is to hold the audience and then, if need be, to rewrite the rules.

In a way, the interesting thing is that, at this point in his career and in the history of serious drama in France, he should engage in this elaborate defense—and in some cases, condemnation—of his own works. He knows that some of his audience or his readers of 1660 expect that kind of thing; they are so absorbed in questions of art that go beyond the immediate experience of works that essays and analyses are needed supplements as he publishes his dramatic texts. Beginning with *Sertorius* (1662), Corneille wrote no more *examens;* although he promised his publisher that when the next group of eight plays was ready, he would supply a fourth discourse and a new group of *examens.* The promise was not kept. Part of the explanation lies, no doubt, in the general movement of taste away from the faith in rules that was so noticeable in and around the Academy during the first years of its existence; and another reason for this silence must lie in the fact that Corneille had won his case against the *doctes* and had given added impetus to the movement in question.

In summary we may say that Corneille considers the pleasure of his audience, or of the majority of it, as the crucial factor in any judgment of his works. If a learned minority wishes to find against him, he is ready and willing to state a position that makes his practice understandable in terms of rules, of course, but also in terms of French usages and of progress by experiment.

"Et nous, qui travaillons pour plaire au public . . . , " writes Racine, in dedicating *Andromaque* to Madame: like Corneille, he aims to please; that rule comes first. The others may be discussed later (if, indeed, at all—Racine has no taste for detailed and public statements about his art). The whole sentence reads: "Et nous, qui travaillons pour plaire au public, nous n'avons plus que faire de demander aux savants si nous travaillons selon les règles. La règle souveraine est de plaire à Votre Altesse Royale" (II, 32).[6] He returns to the theme with a slight variation, as he comments on simplicity in the plot of *Bérénice*. He had sought this quality, but certain people reproached him for it, even though they had been strongly affected by the play and would gladly see it again.

Que veulent-ils davantage? Je les conjure d'avoir assez bonne opinion d'eux-mêmes pour ne pas croire qu'une pièce qui les touche et qui leur donne du plaisir puisse être absolument contre les règles. La principale règle est de plaire et de toucher. Toutes les autres ne sont faites que pour parvenir à cette première. [II, 368.]

And yet, in spite of the repetition of terms that have a Cornelian ring, I wonder if it is not necessary to discount them in Racine's case. I suspect that the audience, that is, the particular group of spectators and patrons for whom he wrote, appeared often to him as a necessary evil. He is aware of the public at large, painfully aware of certain critics, and respectfully, at times snobbishly, aware of the court and the King. He obviously senses and responds in one way or another, positively or negatively, to a *goût du siècle*. A well-known instance may be found in his remarks on the characters of Andromaque and Pyrrhus. He suppresses the second marriage of Andromaque to Molossus: "J'ai cru en cela me conformer à l'idée que nous avons maintenant de cette princesse" (II, 38). We have seen this sort of adjustment before as part of Corneille's technique. But Racine does not hesitate to depart from contemporary taste. Whereas Corneille seems in his second discourse to envy the freedom of the novelist and the ease with which he changes from place to place and stretches his time limits, Racine, when he mentions the novel, comments not on some technical aspect of the art of the genre but on the corruption of taste (he thus turns on the group he professes to wish to please) that has been caused by "precious" characterizations, a corruption that blinds some, at least, to the authenticity of a character like Pyrrhus.

This is symptomatic of a tendency that reverses the emphasis we have noted in Corneille, who on occasion argues from the idea of a typical public while writing for a particular and evolving one. Racine, on the other hand, certainly knows his seventeenth-century audience, but he is inclined to distrust it and to quarrel with it; he actually writes for a generalized and even idealized public that is his own creation. There are two interesting examples of the effort to generalize. In answering a possible objection to some extravagances in *Les Plaideurs* (1668), he says:

Mais enfin je traduis Aristophane, et l'on doit se souvenir qu'il avait affaire à des spectateurs assez difficiles. Les Athéniens savaient apparemment ce que c'était que le sel attique; et ils étaient bien sûrs, quand il avaient ri d'une chose, qu'ils n'avaient pas ri d'une sottise. . . . Quoiqu'il en soit, je puis dire que notre siècle n'a pas été de plus mauvaise humeur que le sien, et que si le but de ma comédie était de faire rire, jamais comédie n'a mieux attrapé son but. [II, 142–43.]

The assimilation and, hence, the generalization are clear. Racine thinks of himself as having written for a group of people who have tastes in common with those of the ancient Greeks and who have in a sense escaped from their own limits in time and space. He returns to this comparison of his French audience to that of classical Athens in the Preface to *Iphigénie* (1674). After mentioning some ways in which he had departed from the tragedy of Euripides, he tells us that, where the passions are concerned, he has followed his model more exactly, with moving results.

J'ai reconnu avec plaisir, par l'effet qu'a produit sur notre théâtre tout ce que j'ai imité ou d'Homère ou d'Euripide, que le bon sens et la raison étaient les mêmes dans tous les siècles. Le goût de Paris s'est trouvé conforme à celui d'Athènes. Mes spectateurs ont été émus des mêmes choses qui ont mis autrefois en larmes le plus savant peuple de la Grèce. . . . [III, 142–43.]

The characteristics that make a good audience—*bon sens, raison, goût*—do not vary, and it is the abstract audience thus constituted that Racine respects and serves.

He also idealizes his audience, in the sense that he tries to define and locate one that is perfectly sensitive, intelligent, and impartial: in view of the prestige associated with antiquity in general and with the Greeks in particular, the passages just quoted are in themselves signs of that tendency. But the process of idealization shows up most clearly after passages in which Racine has felt himself on the defensive. I am thinking especially of the combative tone that one detects in the prefaces to *Britannicus* and *Bérénice,* and, also, though to a lesser degree, in those to *Alexandre* and *Andromaque.* In similar circumstances Corneille presents the figure of the disinterested judge, trying the merits of particular cases against poetic rules, liberally understood. Racine's approach differs completely. He can be quite bitter, as in the first two instances I have mentioned. He is not in the least inclined to start an elaborate exposé of his poetics; he limits himself to quick strokes, rich in implications, such as the following: " . . . Une action simple, chargée de peu de matière, telle que doit être une action qui se passe en un seul jour, et qui s'avançant par degrés vers sa fin, n'est soutenue que par les intérêts, les sentiments et les passions des personnages . . . " (*Britannicus,* Première Préface, II, 246). Or this, which defines so well the general effect that Racine wishes to produce: "Ce n'est point une nécessité qu'il y ait du sang et des morts dans une tragédie: il suffit que l'action en soit grande, que les acteurs en soient héroïques, que les passions y soient excitées, et que tout se ressente de cette tristesse majestueuse qui fait tout le plaisir de la tragédie" (*Bérénice,* Préface, II, 366).

However, these valuable sketches are embedded in paragraphs of sometimes intemperate remarks against the partisans of plots filled with "jeux de théâtre," with improbable incidents and declamations. He is apt to call such critics ignorant and unjust, as when he invokes Terence at the end of the Preface to *Britannicus:* "Homine imperito nunquam quidquam injustius," a line which he had already translated earlier, "Il n'y a rien de plus injuste qu'un ignorant." He refuses to be drawn into a contest with theoreticians who are mainly supporters of Corneille, anyway, and whose poor taste is made worse by ill will. Near the end of the Preface to *Bérénice,* he takes up criticisms offered by certain persons apparently too highly placed to be treated roughly; he suggests that they are misguided rather than ignorant. Their charge had been that a tragedy such as *Bérénice,* with so little complication in its plot, could hardly be composed according to the rules of the theater. Racine's characteristic reaction is to inquire (indirectly, it seems) whether the play had been boring to them. On finding out that, on the contrary, they had been pleased and moved by it, he asks "Que veulent-ils davantage?"

> La principale règle est de plaire et de toucher. Toutes les autres ne sont faites que parvenir à cette première. Mais toutes ces règles sont d'un long détail, dont je ne leur conseille pas [à ces quelques personnes] de s'embarrasser. Ils ont des occupations plus importantes. Qu'ils se reposent sur nous de la fatigue d'éclaircir les difficultés de la *Poétique* d'Aristote; qu'ils se réservent le plaisir de pleurer et d'être attendris; et qu'ils me permettent de leur dire ce qu'un musicien disait à Philippe, roi de Macédoine, qui prétendait qu'une chanson n'était pas selon les règles: "A Dieu ne plaise, Seigneur, que vous soyez si malheureux que de savoir ces choses-là mieux que moi!" [II, 368.]

My point is this: the seventeenth-century poet has two choices in facing his critics; he may answer them by appealing to poetic principles taken as true, or by appealing to other judges in whose opinions one may have more confidence, that is, to the truly qualified part of his audience; Corneille prefers the first alternative, Racine the second. As soon as one gets beyond a few general points that should be clear to everyone, Racine believes poetics to be the business of the poet, not of the spectator, and so, in order to confirm the value of his work, he looks to the reactions of certain elite elements in his audience.

He speaks in the first Preface to *Alexandre* of the approbation of "les premières personnes de la terre et les Alexandres de notre siècle," and in the epistle, addressed to the king, he says delicately that the king "had not disapproved" of his tragedy. *Andromaque* is dedicated to Madame. The movement of thought in the epistle is typical of Racine: away from the negative subtleties of critics to the positive judgments of people of taste. The interest of Madame in the play, her help in composing it, the fact that she had "honored it with tears" when he read it to her for the first time—all that consoled him for the hardness of those who were untouched by it: "Je leur permets de condamner l'*Andromaque* tant qu'ils voudront, pourvu qu'il me soit permis d'appeler de toutes les subtilités de leur esprit au coeur de Votre Altesse Royale" (II, 31). The next paragraph praises her intelligence, and the whole development leads to the statement that the supreme rule is to please Her Majesty. But the elite consists of more than one or two top people. In presenting his next play, *Les Plaideurs,* Racine shows us *la cour* correcting errors of judgment committed in *la ville.* When it was first performed in Paris, there were some who thought it irregular and others who felt that legal subjects would not do as sources of diversion for the court. "La pièce fut bientôt après jouée à Versailles. On ne fit point de scrupule de s'y réjouir; et ceux qui avaient cru se déshonorer de rire à Paris, furent peut-être obligés de rire à Versailles pour se faire honneur" (II, 141).

One cannot, of course, suppose that Racine identified sound taste blindly with Louis XIV, Henriette-Anne d'Angleterre, or some circle at the court. The essential thing is that his mind usually turns, in the face of conflicts and criticisms, to *some* ideal spectator or spectators, and one incarnation of the ideal is found in Versailles and its principal personnages. More significant, no doubt, and more indicative of his true feelings is the extraordinary passage in the Preface to *Britannicus* in which he makes a series of scarcely veiled allusions to some Cornelian heroes and heroines of whom he disapproves, ending on a sarcastic note: "Voilà sans doute de quoi faire récrier tous ces Messieurs." He suggests that he might do likewise, and then he asks two important questions: "Mais que dirait cependant le petit nombre de gens sages auxquels je m'efforce de plaire? De quel front oserais-je me montrer, pour ainsi dire, aux yeux de ces grands hommes de l'antiquité que j'ai choisis pour modèles?" (II, 247). Racine's imagination moves from the small number of contemporaries whose approval really counts with him to an even more select group, great creators in fact, but here changed into spectators and judges. (The idea is no doubt traceable to a passage in chapter xii of Longinus' treatise *On the Sublime*, though Racine does not name his source.) He continues: "Car, pour me servir de la pensée d'un ancien, voilà les véritables spectateurs que nous devons nous proposer; et nous devons sans cesse nous demander: 'Que diraient Homère et Virgile, s'ils lisaient ces vers? que dirait Sophocle, s'il voyait représenter cette scène?'" (II, 248). This climaxes the trend of Racine's thought away from the conception that we noticed in the thinking of Corneille, the conception of an audience given *hic et nunc* and accepted as it is. Racine likes the idea of moving Paris in the direction of Athens, or, at another moment, he will define for himself an audience that can exist only in abstract thought, because, with its good sense and good taste, it is the same everywhere and always.[7] The process of generalization is completed by a tendency to restrict and to idealize the audience. The perfect judges consist of a small number of *gens sages* or of cultivated personnages like Madame and Louis XIV, or, better still, of ideal poet-spectators like one or more of the great ancients.

With *Phèdre* (1677) Racine takes leave of his audience, in the sense of a sizeable and diverse public. When he comes back to dramatic poetry at the request of Mme de Maintenon and creates *Esther* (1689), he is, indeed, working for a select few (and for a very special theater and troupe). The success of the work at Saint Cyr was a brilliant one:

De sorte qu'un divertissement d'enfants est devenu le sujet de l'empressement de toute la cour; le Roi lui-même, qui en avait été touché, n'ayant pu refuser à tout ce qu'il y a de plus grands seigneurs de les y mener, et ayant eu la satisfaction de voir, par le plaisir qu'ils y ont pris, qu'on se peut aussi bien divertir aux choses de piété qu'à tous les spectacles profanes. [II, 456.]

Although Racine the courtier obviously enjoyed this success, something deeper was at stake. It seems certain that his piety had led him by this time away from the concern with pleasing an audience as he had tried to do with *Andromaque* or with *Iphigénie*. After all, there is a new and transcendent Spectator to be reckoned with: "Tout respire ici Dieu . . . ," announces the allegorical personnage, Piety, at the end of the prologue to *Esther*. Have we not here a Racine close enough to Pascal in disposition and outlook to feel in his turn that "le fini s'anéantit en présence de l'infini, et devient un pur néant?"

What he had in mind for *Athalie*, as regards performance and audience, is even more difficult to fathom. It did not have the reception that its predecessor had had, partly because *Esther* had been too successful and had disrupted the program at Saint Cyr, but only partly. Actually, we cannot conceive of a seventeenth-century theater or company or audience that could have done justice to it. *Athalie* represents the final break with any simple notions of *plaire* and *toucher*, of subservience to details of performance and to verdicts of spectators; and it thus reveals in retrospect, I believe, the real and profound sense of Racine's relation to his audience throughout his career. The persistent desire to universalize it and to idealize it that we have noted is actually his means of freeing himself from the limits and dangers of a rhetorical conception of tragedy. There can be no doubt that his art owes a great deal to the principles and discipline of rhetoric, but these things are means to poetic ends with him; in reality, he is haunted far more by form and thought

159

than by effect. One cannot say that the audience is his guide as he finds his way from *Andromaque* to *Phèdre* and the perfected tragic form animating it or from *Esther* to *Athalie,* two steps in the evolution of another dramatic form. Racine knows better than anyone else what he wants to do and what his ideal is; he knows it because he works, not from sensitivity to the reigning taste, but from familiarity with great models.

In the series of works from *Andromaque* to *Phèdre,* he strives for the particular synthesis and proper ordering of action, character, thought, and style, for the simplicity and elegance that had been " . . . si fort du goût des anciens" (II, 36). And, as he explains it, he hopes to achieve in his last two plays two other characteristics of his Greek models. In the first place, he tries to integrate chorus and music into his dramas, so as to realize more fully the possibilities inherent in an art that is directed to performance; and, in the second place, on an other than technical plane, he dares to integrate drama with religion, as his models had done (with this difference, of course, that their basis had been pagan, while his is Christian). Racine seeks at this late moment in his career to resolve the conflict, long standing in his century, between drama and faith, between experience in the theater and the rest of one's experience, colored as it must be by Christian habits and convictions. He attempts to bring about by a creative stroke what was a *datum* for the ancients, since their drama was not far from its origins in religion. He says the whole thing very simply:

J'entrepris donc la chose [la composition d'*Esther*], et je m'aperçus qu'en travaillant sur le plan qu'on m'avait donné, j'exécutais en quelque sorte un dessein qui m'avait souvent passé dans l'esprit, qui était de lier, comme dans les anciennes tragédies grecques, le choeur et le chant avec l'action, et d'employer à chanter les louanges du vrai Dieu cette partie du choeur que les païens employaient à chanter les louanges de leurs fausses divinités. [III, 455.]

In short, what Racine wanted all the time to do, apparently, was to achieve a more and more authentic revival of an ancient genre, and the stages of that re-creation correspond roughly to stages in his personal evolution. As a poet he depended less and less on his audience; his light came from other sources—from form at first and then, also, from Christian truth as he saw and understood it.

Of the three great seventeenth-century dramatists, Molière has the most intimate acquaintance with his public. Racine tends to write for an ideal audience, one that has never been and never can be fully and concretely realized. Corneille writes for a real audience, and yet he keeps a certain moral distance between it and him. But Molière, whose energies are so completely bound up in the theater, has to know his spectators and their tastes. His contact with them as manager and as member of a troupe is necessarily very close. He must know them, moreover, for reasons arising from the nature of comedy.

A glance back at a statement made by Racine will show by contrast the principle involved. In the "Seconde préface" to *Bajazet*, he justifies himself carefully for starting from a subject that is nearly contemporary, the main episodes of the story having taken place in Constantinople about thirty years before. He would not recommend, he says, choosing such a subject if the action had taken place in the country of the spectators, where the principal characters would be, if not familiar, at least known to them. "Les personnages tragiques doivent être regardés d'un autre oeil que nous ne regardons d'ordinaire les personnages que nous avons vus de si près. On peut dire que le respect que l'on a pour les héros augmente à mesure qu'ils s'éloignent de nous: *major e longinquo reverentia*" (II, 477). To produce its proper effect, tragedy must

161

start from people and acts that are remote; and Racine's argument is, precisely, that Turks in Constantinople are sufficiently remote, in place at least, to satisfy this primary condition. If there is to be tragedy in the Racinian manner, the dramatist must see events and characters *e longinquo* and make it possible for his audience to do the same. Molière obviously thinks of comedy and its subject matter in exactly the opposite way: he takes it as a *miroir public* that is focussed on surrounding and identifiable realities. Consequently, his view of the audience has a special ambiguity.

As *spectators*, he sees them in the light of the ever-recurring notion of *plaire*. In the *Critique de l'école des femmes*, Lysidas, the pedantic poet, provokes Dorante, the defender of Molière, to the following classic retort: "Je voudrais bien savoir si la grande règle de toutes les règles n'est pas de plaire, et si une pièce de théâtre qui a attrapé son but n'a pas suivi un bon chemin" (III, 358).[8] He returns to the point a few lines later: "Je dis bien que le grand art est de plaire, et que cette comédie ayant plu à ceux pour qui elle est faite, je trouve que c'est assez pour elle et qu'elle doit peu se soucier du reste" (III, 360). However, and this is where the ambiguity begins, Molière sees his audience also as his *subject matter,* as a basic element in the maneuvers of comic creation. His specific task is, he says, to " . . . entrer comme il faut dans le ridicule des hommes, et de rendre agréablement sur le théâtre les défauts de tout le monde" (III, 351). Or, in the same vein: "Lorsque vous peignez les hommes, il faut peindre d'après nature; on veut que ces portraits ressemblent, et vous n'avez rien fait si vous n'y faites reconnaître les gens de votre siècle" (III, 354). Molière hopes to observe and represent in such a way as to cause in the theater an experience of recognition, and sometimes of self-recognition, of truth and its applications: that is, I believe, the force of the *castigat ridendo* for him. In order to please his audience, Molière must, therefore, put it into his work, with due attention, of course, to the first principle of comic art, according to which one does not represent individuals (that went out, as Boileau was to recall in the *Art poétique*, with the end of the old Greek comedy) but comic natures. They are abstract, but, by that very token, communicable to many.

What happens when Molière reacts against unfavorable judgments to his audience or of some segment of it? "Segment" seems the proper word, because he enjoys on the whole, as Corneille does, a relationship of mutual sympathy with the people who come to his plays. When attacked, however, he does not defend himself, in the manner of Corneille, on the basis of rules and art. On this subject Molière's attitude resembles that of Racine: he appeals incidentally and reluctantly to rules. Dorante's reply to Lycidas, which I have quoted earlier, gives Molière's view—that his work does, in fact, conform to the "rules," since it pleases the public for which it was created. By this argument he empties the rules of all their mystery and most of their prescriptive force. They become, as Dorante goes on to say, " . . . quelques observations aisées que le bon sens a faites sur ce qui peut ôter le plaisir que l'on prend à ces sortes de poèmes; et le même bon sens qui a fait autrefois ces observations les fait aisément tous les jours sans le secours d'Horace et d'Aristote" (III, 358). They are found empirically, and are easily rediscovered; they are guidelines and guardrails, helpful in knowing what should be left out rather than what should be put in. Like Corneille, then, Molière knows that he can fall back on the favor of the audience as one answer to his critics.

The curious thing is that when he addresses himself more specifically to the critics in order to remind them that they are in the minority, he does not write prefaces and discourses. The great exception comes in the quarrel over *Tartuffe*, but that does not really invalidate the point, I think: Molière's more natural reaction is to offer plays in his defense. He prefers not to set aside his comic vision in dealing with critics, for that vision may and does include his public, his critics, and even himself. Here, as elsewhere in his comedies, his satirical technique is directed *ad hominem*, or, more exactly, perhaps, *ad naturam*: what a man says is linked inseparably to that man's nature or basic moral disposition. It is one of the axioms of Molière's art that the sense and value of words and actions are fixed ultimately by the mental and moral character of the agent. This insight, brilliantly illustrated by complex creations like Tartuffe and Alceste but notable as well in many lesser figures, inspires him as he begins to deal with critics. He relates what people say about the *Ecole des femmes* to their characters, thereby recalling to the more intelligent part of his audience that the detractors are pedants, *envieux, prudes, précieux, marquis*. The moral essences that determine what they do and say are enough to disqualify them as judges. To complete his response, Molière makes it possible for the men of good sense to identify themselves with reasonable spokesmen like Dorante and the Chevalier, who belong to the line of Philinte (in *Le Misanthrope*), Cléante (in *Tartuffe*), and Chrysalde (in the *Ecole des femmes*).

The principles are the same when Molière answers his attackers directly instead of representing them: in the Préface to *Tartuffe*, he emphasizes to us and to his contemporary readers the vicious morality that underlies the criticisms and then appeals on rational grounds to the better part of his audience: "Ils n'ont eu garde de l'attaquer [la comédie] par le côté qui les a blessés: ils sont trop politiques pour cela et savent trop bien vivre pour découvrir le fond de leur âme. Suivant leur louable coutume, ils ont couvert leurs intérêts de la cause de Dieu: et *le Tartuffe*, dans leur bouche est une pièce qui offense la piété" (IV, 373). Their behavior in

164

connection with the play is in character; it harmonizes with the rest of their actions. As for the audience that is real for Molière, the one that he respects, these lines occur just below the preceding ones:

J'ai eu beau la soumettre [la comédie] aux lumières de mes amis et à la censure de tout le monde: les corrections que j'ai pu faire, le jugement du Roi et de la Reine, qui l'ont vue, l'approbation des grands Princes et de Messieurs les Ministres, qui l'ont honorée de leur présence, le témoignage des gens de bien, qui l'ont trouvée profitable, tout cela n'a rien servi. [IV, 374.]

Let us return for a moment to the *Critique*. Speaking in the first secene of her love of company and visitors, which has just been condemned by Elise, Uranie explains very briefly: "Je goûte ceux qui sont raisonnables et me divertis des extravagants" (III, 312). Is this not the key to Molière's conception of his audience, whether he views it as a source of subjects or as a group of spectators? Working on the plane of comic creation, he locates among them the *extravagants* who are to be his targets, and then, on the other plane, that of the spectators and their experiences in the theater, he assumes that *every one* will recognize the truth of his characterizations and that his *comic models* will move in some small degree out of their errors, flaws, and rigidities. If the latter protest instead, Molière's characteristic impulse is to *re*-represent them so that the healthy part of his public is confirmed in its judgment and the other part is abandoned to its particular form of the ridiculous.

In these texts we see three distinct conceptions of the audience; and, since the dramatists all accept (at least initially) as an underlying rule that the audience is entitled to be pleased, we also see three distinct ways of keeping this principle from becoming too burdensome. Corneille thinks of himself as facing a particular group of people whose taste is a matter of a given historical moment; he willingly accepts the decision of the many; for the learned few he supplies reasons for many aspects of his practice, arguing from a precise but undogmatic view of his art. Racine thinks of himself as facing an audience containing a goodly number of ignorant and prejudiced people whose taste cannot be taken as the final criterion; he, therefore, tends to re-create it by broadening it to take in people of other ages, or he introduces important divisions into it. He prefers to see himself as working for the court, or for a few *gens sages*, or for the great ancients, who can be invoked at least in his imagination, or, finally, by an unexpected turn, for Saint Cyr and God. He will reason from artistic principles on occasion; but if one compares the sum of what he has to say about his dramatic technique with the sum of Corneille's criticism, there is no doubt that he expressed his real view when he quoted, apropos of *Bérénice*, the reply of the musician to Philip of Macedon. With Molière there is nothing like Racine's effort to find somehow and somewhere the audience he ought to have; he thinks of himself as facing a particular audience that is basically won over, that is already his, with the exception of a few of his targets. After that statement, however, one must elaborate a bit: there is the rather undifferentiated but very much prized group of sensible people that includes the court;[9] on the other hand, there is the large and variegated group of people, particularly noticeable to Molière when he is author rather than actor,[10] who are irrational in one way or another. If he is criticized, he resorts even less than Racine does to statements of principles, once the general thesis of comedy as the *miroir public* has been advanced; he merely turns his art on his attackers.

Seventeenth-century literary theory tended, with few exceptions, to crown a *situation de fait*, in which the Molières, Racines, and Corneilles, real or fancied, were dependent on audiences and protectors. Its typical reflex, so to speak, was to discuss literary art in terms of the rhetorical triad—poet, work, and audience—so adjusted to each other that the special weight of the third factor does not nullify the other two. What we see in the prefaces, discourses, and critical plays examined here is a constant effort on the part of poets to make this system work, either by insisting on distinctions and refinements in the audience or by showing that any drama called into question conforms in fact to recognized conventions and truths of poetics.

1. *Oeuvres de P. Corneille,* ed. Charles Marty-Laveaux ("Grands Ecrivains de la France" [Paris, 1862–68]), I, 72. All quotations in the text have been taken from this edition.

2. *Ibid.,* III, 94. For another and similar instance, see *ibid.,* IV, 138, where, apropos of *Le Menteur,* he tells us of changing the ending of *La Verdad sospechosa* so that, in accordance with the French convention of his day, there would be a happy outcome for everyone in the play.

3. G. Couton, *Réalisme de Corneille* (Paris, 1953).

4. The lines from Terence are: "Poeta, quum primum animum ad scribendum appulit, / Id sibi negoti credidit solum dari / Populo ut placeret, quas fecisset fabulas" (*Andria,* Prologue, 1–3). ("When the poet first applied his mind to writing, he supposed that his sole business was to see that his plays pleased the people.")

5. *Ars poetica,* 286–87, and Epistles I. xix. 19.

6. All of my references are to *Oeuvres de J. Racine,* ed. Paul Mesnard ("Grands Ecrivains de la France" [Paris, 1865–73]).

7. One might expect, therefore, some mention of future generations as well as of past and present ones. Racine cannot have been indifferent to the judgment of posterity, but I have found only one reference to it in the prefaces and *épîtres,* and that one is rather oblique. Apropos of *Phèdre,* he writes: "Au reste, je n'ose encore assurer que cette pièce soit en effet la meilleure de mes tragédies. Je laisse et aux lecteurs et au temps à décider de son véritable prix" (II, 302).

8. All references are to *Oeuvres de Molière,* ed. Eugène Despois and Paul Mesnard ("Grands Ecrivains de la France" [Paris, 1873–1900]).

9. "Sachez, s'il vous plaît, Monsieur Lycidas, que les courtisans ont d'aussi bons yeux que d'autres . . . que la grande épreuve de toutes vos comédies, c'est le jugement de la cour; que c'est son goût qu'il faut étudier pour trouver l'art de réussir; qu'il n'y a point de lieu où les décisions soient si justes; . . . que du simple bon sens naturel et du commerce de tout le beau monde, on s'y fait une manière d'esprit qui,

sans comparaison, juge plus finement des choses que tout le savoir en-rouillé des pédants" (*Critique*, III, 354–55). Molière finds a way, a few lines further on, to qualify this sweeping praise of the court. He has Dorante say: "La Cour a quelques ridicules, j'en demeure d'accord, et je suis, comme on voit, le premier à les fronder" (III, 542). See also note 10, below.

10. In the *Impromptu de Versailles,* there is a point at which the chevalier is asked by the marquis whether Molière has exhausted all possible comic subjects. Dorante replies: "Plus de matière? Eh! mon pauvre Marquis, nous lui en fournissons toujours assez. . . . Crois-tu qu'il ait épuisé dans ses comédies tout le ridicule des hommes? Et sans sortir de la Cour, n'a-t-il presque vingt caractères de gens où il n'a point touché. . . . Va, va, Marquis, Molière aura toujours plus de sujets qu'il n'en voudra; et tout ce qu'il a touché jusqu'ici n'est rien que bagatelle au prix de ce qui reste" (III, 415).

Chapter VII

Conclusions and Implications

𝔍 N THE FIRST four chapters of this book I have given an account of the rise of two radically different conceptions of rhetoric and of the clash between them. The first of these, whose history I have outlined by taking as the point of departure the program of the Academy and as the more or less clear denouement the *Comparaisons* and *Réflexions* of Rapin, came into being by a long process in which a theory of expression that goes back to Quintilian and Cicero and through them to Greek theorists was translated, adapted, and reformulated. I have studied the second in the *Logique* of Port-Royal; it has its ancient precedents, too, though not so much in theories of expression as in Greek atomisms and geometry; it came into being in seventeenth-century France as a development and application of the method of Descartes. These two approaches to problems of expression and persuasion are so different that when we study them in the texts where they are stated in pure terms, we must finally see them as incommensurable. But the two theories, with their aspirations toward persuasion, on the one hand, and toward demonstration, on the other, are involved in various fruitful compromises, with the result that the tendency to artifice in the one and to aridity in the other are overcome in a general ambition to be both appealing and truthful in every kind of expression.

In Chapters V and VI, it was possible to show, at least in part, how the two approaches were developed and specified by Pascal and by the most important dramatists of the period. In Pascal we have someone perfectly able to work on two levels, on that of theory as well as that of practice. He has no fully worked-out treatise on the subject of rhetoric, but he does have two significant fragments that outline a treatise; and there are many signs in the *Pensées* of the degree to which he is fascinated by problems of intellectual method. In the *Lettres provinciales* there is much evidence to show that what he chooses to write about as he enters the argument between the Jesuits and the Jansenists and what he takes to be suitable criteria in assaying the truth of the two positions derived from considerations such as those set down in the fragments. In fact, the basic conflict, that between a rhetoric based on appeals to opinions known to be favored by the person addressed (the position of the Ciceronians and of Rapin) and a rhetoric based on objective grounds that must be accepted by the person being addressed (the position of Port-Royal and of Pascal), lies at the heart of Pascal's procedure. The *opinions probables* of the Jesuits and their imperialistic aims which justify any means as long as it is effective—I speak as Pascal might, not as a historian—are treated much as the discipline of rhetoric is treated in the logic of Port-Royal; the victorious point of view is quasi-geometrical in its structure and dynamics. The striking thing is that when Pascal comes to the task that underlies the *Pensées*, he selects a very different technique, one that is dialectical rather than demonstrative in the fashion of geometry. In other words, he not only sides with the Port-Royalists in their opposition to the traditional rhetoric, he also knows how to formulate and use still another procedure when occasion demands.

The example of Pascal (in the *Provinciales*, at least) is that of a man who, by generalizing a mathematical method, arrives at a logic that he can apply to problems of persuasion in apologetics. Corneille, Racine, and Molière certainly were not theoreticians of rhetoric on any comparable scale; they were interested in literary creation rather than in religious conversion or polemic. Still, one finds in what they say to their critics arguments that depend for their force on a conception of dramatic art that must be called rhetorical, it seems to me. This time the technique of "persuasion" is more traditional than Cartesian in inspiration. I have not tried to align the plays or passages from them with the more technical pages of Cicero and Quintilian—as has been done in some studies —in order to locate examples of the various *topoi*, devices, and figures of speech or thought that are treated theoretically in the sources; instead, I have studied the audience as a force in creative consciousness, using as evidence the statements that the playwrights made about what they were doing or thought they had done. The basic problem is this: once one has accepted the rhetorical framework, one must form a precise image of the audience for which one writes and in that act form an idea of oneself and of one's art. Corneille, Racine, and Molière all agree in assuming that the audience is a decisive factor, but for reasons of temperament, personal circumstances, and what may be called generic vocation, each has his own way of coping with it.

"Classique est l'écrivain qui porte un critique en soi-même et qui l'associe intimement à ses travaux." Valéry's definition applies, as a matter of fact, to almost every major writer in France, at least since the Renaissance. If one considers the period covered by the present studies—from 1635 to 1685, roughly speaking—it certainly points to something essential in the consciousness of the principal authors. From the founding of the Academy to the Quarrel of the Ancients and the Moderns, one question with which they worked was the following: in the light of what poetic principles could they bring into existence a literature worthy of France and of its monarchy and worthy of being compared with the classical legacy? This does not mean that they were not as interested as we are in the dilemmas and contradictions of human behavior or that they could not go far beneath the masks that men wore then and in every age; nor does it deny their ability to sense the problems of "human time" or to recognize, with anguish in some cases, the *néant* to which men must return or from which, with supernatural aid, they may hope to escape. What it does mean is that these concerns, though real and present, emerge into a critical consciousness that is focussed on the process of creation. The seventeenth century thought profoundly about man, his nature, and his existence, but experience and reflection alone did not bring into being those works in which we may, at our leisure, see the characteristic humanism of the age. In the presence of this flowering, of this marvelous burst of literary creativity, we must note these truths: *It was essentially contingent, it might not have been, it would not have been but for the force of a productive discipline that caused works to be.*

I am not reverting to the notion of a theoretical and disembodied *doctrine classique*. I am not speaking of a critical system; as the history of criticism in the seventeenth century shows, nothing that can be called a system was ever fully achieved; poetic and rhetorical disciplines functioned as ideal goals while always remaining, in fact, more or less amorphous. On the contrary, I am saying that, as we think about the factors implied by the very existence of French classical literature, we are led not to lifeless doctrine but to personal discipline, to a kind of qualification that has been freely assumed by someone and vitally held by him in view of doing or making something well. Such a personal qualification has, of course, a content; and when that content is made explicit, one slips often into the statement of something like a theory. But the ideological part must always be understood as entering into the powers of a particular writer or poet and as affecting, though not mechanically determining, his creative activity.

Reserving for the moment further comment on the *subjective* aspect of discipline so understood, let us summarize its *objective* content as that emerges from the preceding studies.

1. In the first place, we have been discussing knowledge directed to the uses of language. That is not its only subject matter; the revivals of the Ciceronian tradition during the seventeenth century were accompanied by an effort to recapture a truly comprehensive view of problems of expression; to brake the tendency to associate rhetoric with only one of its parts, the study of style; and to substitute for that narrow view a conception of the art as dealing also with the invention and arrangement of ideas and arguments and with the characteristics and interests of audiences. One of the important complaints of the Port-Royalists was that the "style rhétoricien" reflected an excessive concern with words and an inclination to let ideas and things slip toward the edges of the inquiry. Still, language is rarely out of sight, for the simple reason that it looks both ways: backward to the meaning that it conveys and forward, as the proximate cause, to the effect being sought. There is no need to dwell here on the work done in the seventeenth century to purify and to temper the French language so that it would be capable of all kinds of eloquence, but the acceptance of the linguistic medium as distinctive and self-contained is noteworthy. Terms derived from the plastic arts or from music do not invade in any significant way the discussions of literature. In fact, several signs point in the opposite direction: it is argued that pictures must have their equivalents of the three unities; drawing and

color are for the Port-Royalists ways of illustrating the distinction between thought and figurative expression; Poussin studies Quintilian.

2. According to the plan of the Academy, verbal disciplines —once the *Dictionnaire* was out of the way—would be expounded under the three headings of grammar, rhetoric, and poetics. Within this framework, however, they intended to give eloquence or rhetoric a special place. As the *Remarques* of Vaugelas show, it is the discipline into which grammar flows, so to speak, and out of which poetics arises as the resources of language are used in a freer and richer way. The priority of rhetoric is even more marked in the theory of Rapin, where the field of belles-lettres is divided into eloquence proper, poetics, history, and philosophy. As is clear from the analyses given in the second chapter above, the first of these not only provides the basis for the others but many themes and devices characteristic of rhetoric turn up in the reflections assigned to the other disciplines.

3. The subordination of poetics to rhetoric implies at once a certain attitude toward the audience, whether it is composed of readers or listeners or spectators. In a theory (such as that of Aristotle) where poetics has an independent status, the poet or writer works with the primary aim of bringing into being a concrete whole or a self-affirming object; that creation is the end of his labor, not what someone will think of what he has done. If the audience is in his mind, it is there as an indirect influence; and he tends to think of it in average or perhaps in ideal terms; it is not particularized. In a poetic theory that is polarized by rhetoric, however, the writer is concerned from the beginning with the effect on his readers or spectators, because success or failure with the members of that audience is an immediate sign of the value of his work. And he has to cope with his public as it is, here and now.

174

Corneille, Racine, and Molière knew this, as their critical writings make clear: although each of them had his own way of defending himself against this *force majeure*—withdrawal when one no longer had an effective rapport with it, appeal over its head to an elite or to an imaginary jury of ancients, appeal to Louis XIV or to the majority of the audience—each of them was conscious of writing for a small group of particular people, made up for the most part of well-to-do bourgeois, real and would-be aristocrats, the king and his entourage. Moreover, in a more or less pure theory of poetics, the effect produced by a work depends on the unique combination of materials and form that it realizes; in other words, the effect inheres in the work. Where rhetoric tends to dominate thinking about poetry, the end of expression lies outside itself in persuasion, an event that takes place in the audience, not in the work. I should add that seventeenth-century poets do not often think of themselves as trying to persuade; however, they almost invariably associate their works with effects that in ancient times were taken to be secondary aims of the orator: *delectare* or *conciliare, docere,* and *movere,* which become *plaire, instruire,* and *émouvoir.*

4. Beyond the idea of verbal discipline in general and the conception of rhetoric as the main verbal discipline, we may take note of more particular questions, such as those having to do with genres and rules. We all know that, to the strict seventeenth-century theorists at least, there is a nicely graded hierarchy from the epic to the epigram and that each of these has its requirements of action or thought or emotion and style. What we do not see so clearly is that these differentiations in works are related to the other two factors involved in the rhetorical process: audience and author. The audience for an epic is not in the same state of mind or expectation as the audience for an epigram, nor is the audience for a comedy

identical, descriptively speaking, to that for a tragedy. We note comparable differences when we turn to eloquence in prose: there is *l'éloquence de la chaire, l'éloquence du barreau*, and the eloquence proper to the councils of the Prince (a feeble copy of the deliberative sort described by Aristotle and practiced by Cicero); and each of these has its particular audience. Again, poets are constantly being urged to consult their forces, to know themselves, to find the type of inspiration to which they are subject, and to study and practice the corresponding types of writing. My point is that the generic distinctions used by the seventeenth-century critics and writers may be explained in part, as they usually are, by reference to what Aristotle and Horace and their commentators had said and in part, no doubt, by the natural tendency of the human mind to see things as instances of types; but whatever their origin, they became enmeshed in the consequences of rhetorical principles and their precise meanings were fixed by the interrelations of artists, works, and audiences.

It is at this point that the literary implications of these studies become clear. If it is true, as I have assumed, that many —even most—of the principal seventeenth-century authors sought to create for their own time a great literature, it is also true that they intended to do this without neglecting the claims of art and reason. They exemplify very well the definition of Valéry: each of them was to some degree, and usually to a high degree, a critic; while doing what he did, he wanted to know why he was doing it. I am suggesting that if we raise our eyes from the works and study the productive conditions that surrounded them as they were being elaborated, we find ourselves facing, along with accidents (but how *necessary* they are!) of circumstance and genius, an impressive ensemble of ideas. I have not presented it as a system, as a "classical doctrine," or as a list of rules. It has a certain shape, though the outlines are vague and the distinctions ambiguous;

and it has an objective existence. However, this ensemble is particularly interesting when we take into account its subjective aspect and its presence in the mind of the classical artist, for that is where it has an effective mode of being. There it forms the technical background against which he makes many of his choices. Placed from the beginning in the perspective of efficient causality, he sees himself as one who works entirely or for the most part with words, not with words chosen for self-expression alone, nor with words used as the matter of an art object, but with words as part of a performance or a transaction. He writes for a public situation in which there will be a sequence of things done, said, known, and felt. As for the rules governing the game, since they now bear his mark and have become part of his creative power, he sees them as hints, vitally grasped, of possible plans and effects. He is aware of himself as *free within limits*. Although he did not invent the limits, he has chosen what his attitude toward them will be. For the most part he accepts them because of the challenges and promises that they hold out to him, but he knows that he may have to set himself new bounds beyond the old.

In the adventures of rhetoric in seventeenth-century France, the historian of ideas and methods uncovers, therefore, the results of a persistent attempt to renew and rebuild one of the great intellectual techniques invented by the ancients, and to do so, furthermore, in the face of attacks from expert controversialists for whom the future belonged to logic. The historian of literature finds in the documents principles of interest to him, for they make it possible for him to see in criticism now three centuries old signs of life and coherence instead of a curious taste for arbitrary pronouncements. It opens up to him, moreover, an important factor in some of the great creative

minds of the century. In several ways and degrees this rhetorical discipline was actualized in the energies of Pascal,
Corneille, Racine, and Molière. That it played a part in their
ways of stating and solving their problems is no doubt the
surest testimony to its power and greatness; that some of their
contemporaries misconceived and misapplied it should not
cause us to undervalue its role, although their failures do make
clear to us the essential misery of rhetoric, which is that it
must always wait upon intelligence and inspiration.

A Selected Bibliography

I. Primary Sources

ARNAULD, A. and NICOLE, P. *La Logique ou l'art de penser.* 2nd ed.; Paris, 1664 [1st ed., 1662].

ARNAULD, A. *Réflexions sur l'éloquence des prédicateurs.* Paris, 1695.

AUBIGNAC, FRANÇOIS HÉDELIN, ABBÉ D'. *Discours académique sur l'éloquence.* . . . Paris, 1668.

———. *Essais d'éloquence chrétienne.* Paris, 1671.

BALZAC, J. L. GUEZ DE. *Les Oeuvres diverses du Sr. de Balzac.* Paris, 1644.

BARY, R. *Actions publiques sur la rhétorique française.* Paris, 1658.

———. *La Rhétorique française.* Paris, 1659.

———. *Nouveau journal de conversations sur toutes les actions publiques des prédicateurs.* Paris, 1675.

———. *Méthode pour bien prononcer un discours et le bien animer.* Paris, 1679.

BOUHOURS, D. *Entretiens d'Ariste et d'Eugène,* ed. R. RADOUANT. Paris, 1920 [1st ed., 1671].

———. *La Manière de bien penser dans les ouvrages d'esprit.* Paris, 1687.

BOISSIMON, DE. *Les Beautés de l'ancienne éloquence opposées aux affectations de la moderne.* Paris, 1698.

BRETON, N. *De la rhétorique selon les préceptes d'Aristote, de Cicéron et de Quintilien.* Paris, 1703.

BRETTEVILLE, ETIENNE DUBOIS, ABBÉ DE. *L'Eloquence de la chaire et du barreau.* Paris, 1689.

BRULART DE SILLERY, FABIO; LAMY, DOM FRANÇOIS; and ARNAULD, A. *Réflexions sur l'éloquence.* Paris, 1700.

CAREL DE SAINTE-GARDE, J. *Réflexions académiques sur les orateurs et sur les poètes.* Paris, 1676.

COLLETET, G. *L'Art poétique du Sr. Colletet.* Paris, 1658.

DUBOIS-GOIBAUD, P. *Les Sermons de S. Augustin.* . . . Paris, 1694.

FÉNELON, B. DE LA MOTHE-. *Dialogues sur l'éloquence en général . . . avec une lettre écrite à l'Académie française.* Paris, 1718.

FOIX, LE PÈRE M. A. DE. *L'Art de prêcher la parole de Dieu.* Paris, 1687.

GAULTIER, C. *Les Plaidoyers.* Paris, 1662.

GILBERT, B. *De la véritable éloquence.* . . . Paris, 1703.

———. *Réflexions sur la rhétorique, où l'on répond aux objections du P. Lamy, Bénédictin.* Paris, 1705.

———. *Jugements des savants sur les auteurs qui ont traité de la rhétorique.* . . . 3 vols. Paris, 1713–19.

GUÉRET, G. *Entretiens sur l'éloquence de la chaire et du barreau.* Paris, 1666.

———. *Le Parnasse réformé.* Paris, 1669.

———. *La Guerre des auteurs anciens et modernes.* La Haye, 1671.

———. *L'Orateur.* Paris, 1672.

———; and RACAN, H. DE BUEIL DE; et al. ? *Divers traités d'histoire, de morale et d'éloquence.* Paris, 1672.

HAUTEVILLE, N. DE. *L'Art de bien discourir.* . . . Paris, 1666.

LA MOTHE LE VAYER, F. DE *Considérations sur l'éloquence française de ce temps.* Paris, 1638.

LAMY, LE PÈRE BERNARD. *La Rhétorique ou l'art de parler.* Paris, 1675.

LAMY, DOM FRANÇOIS. *De la connaissance de soi-même.* Paris, 1694.

———. *La Rhétorique de collège trahie par son apologiste.* . . . Paris, 1704. (See GILBERT, B., above.)

LEGRAS, LE SIEUR [MICHEL-ANTOINE?]. *La Rhétorique française.* Paris, 1671.

LE MAISTRE, A. *Les Plaidoyers et harangues.* Paris, 1657.

PATRU, O. *Oeuvres.* 2 vols., Paris, 1714.

PELLISSON-FONTANIER, P., and D'OLIVET, P. J. T. *Histoire de l'Académie française.* 3rd ed.; Paris, 1743.

SAINT-PAUL, LE PÈRE CH. DE. *Tableau de l'éloquence françiase.* . . . Paris, 1657.

RAPIN, R. *Les Comparaisons des grands hommes de l'antiquité.* . . . *Les Réflexions sur l'éloquence, la poétique, l'histoire et la philosophie.* 2 vols. Paris, 1684.

RICHESOURCE, O. DE. *L'Art de bien dire.* Paris, 1662.

————. *L'Eloquence de la chaire ou la rhétorique des prédicateurs.* Paris, 1665.

————. *La Rhétorique du barreau ou la manière de bien plaider.* Paris, 1668.

VAUGELAS, CL. FAVRE DE. *Remarques sur la langue française* . . . , ed. J. STREICHER. Paris, 1934 [1st ed., Paris, 1647].

II. Secondary Sources

ABRAMS, M. H. *The Mirror and the Lamp.* New York, 1953.

ADAM, ANTOINE. *Histoire de la littérature française au XVIIe siècle.* 5 vols. Paris, 1948–56.

AUERBACH, ERICH. "La Cour et la ville," *Vier Untersuchungen zur Geschichte der französischen Bildung.* Bern, 1951. Pp. 12–50.

BOISSIER, G. *L'Académie française sous l'ancien régime.* Paris, 1909.

BORGERHOFF, E. B. O. *The Freedom of French Classicism.* Princeton, 1950.

————. "The Reality of Pascal: The *Pensées* as Rhetoric," *Sewanee Review,* LXV (January–March, 1957), 15–33.

BRAY, RENÉ. *La formation de la doctrine classique.* Paris, 1951.

BRODY, JULES. *Boileau and Longinus.* Geneva, 1958.

BRUNOT, F. *Histoire de la langue française des origines à 1900.* Vols. III–IV. Paris, 1930 and 1939.

COUSIN, JEAN. "Rhétorique latine et classicisme français," *Revue des cours et conférences* (28 February–30 July 1933). Paris, 1933.

CURTIUS, E. R. *European Literature and Latin Middle Ages.* Translated by WILLARD R. TRASK. New York, [1953].

DUBU, J. "De quelques raisons esthétiques du silence de Racine après *Phèdre,*" *Le Dix-septième siècle,* XX (1953), 341–49.

GIRAUDOUX, J. "Racine," *Littérature.* Paris, 1943. Pp. 27–55.

HOWELL, W. S. *Logic and Rhetoric in England.* Princeton, 1956.

KNIGHT, R. C. "The Evolution of Racine's Poétique," *Modern Language Review,* XXXV (1940), 19–39.

———. *Racine et la Grèce.* Paris, 1950.

LANTOINE, H. *Histoire de l'enseignement secondaire en France au XVIIᵉ et au début du XVIIIᵉ siècle.* Paris, 1874.

LAWRENSON, T. E. *The French Stage in the XVIIth Century.* Manchester, 1957.

LOUGH, J. *Paris Theatre Audiences in the Seventeenth and Eighteenth Centuries.* London, 1957.

McKEON, RICHARD. "The Philosophic Bases of Art and Criticism," and "Rhetoric in the Middle Ages," *Critics and Criticism,* ed. R. S. CRANE. Chicago, 1952.

———. *Freedom and History,* New York, 1952.

———. *Thought, Action and Passion.* Chicago, 1954.

———. "Dialogue and Controversy in Philosophy," *Philosophy and Phenomenological Research,* XVII (December, 1956), 143–63.

MAY, G. *Tragédie cornélienne, tragédie racinienne.* Urbana, Ill., 1948.

MOORE, W. G. *Molière: A New Criticism.* Oxford, 1949.

MORNET, D. *Histoire de la clarté française.* Paris, 1929.

MUNTEANO, B. "Survivances antiques: Abbé du Bos, esthéticien de la persuasion passionnelle," *Revue de littérature comparée,* XXX (1956), 318–50.

———. "Humanisme et Rhétorique: la survie littéraire de rhéteurs anciens," *Revue d'histoire littéraire de la France,* LVIII, No. 2 (1958), 145–56.

NELSON, R. J. "*Impromptu de Versailles* Reconsidered," *French Studies,* XI (1957), 305–14.

ORCIBAL, J. *La Genèse d'Esther et d'Athalie.* Paris, 1950.

PEYRE, H. *Le Classicisme français.* New York, 1942.

————. "Le Classicisme," *Encyclopédie de la Pléiade.* (Paris, 1956), II, 111–39.

PICARD, R. *La Carrière de Jean Racine.* Paris, 1956.

SAINTE-BEUVE, C. A. *Port-Royal,* ed. MAXIME LEROY. 3 vols. Paris, 1953–55.

SELLSTROM, A. D. "Rhetoric and the Poetics of French Classicism," *French Review,* XXXIV (1960–61), 425–31.

SOTER, ISTVAN. *La Doctrine stylistique des rhétoriques du XVIIᵉ siècle.* Budapest, 1937.

TOPLISS, P. "Pascal's Theory of Persuasion and Ancient Rhetoric," *Esprit créateur,* II, No. 2 (1962), 79–83.

WEINBERG, B. *A History of Literary Criticism in the Italian Renaissance.* 2 vols. Chicago, 1961.

Index